Eyewitness
PREHISTORIC
LIFE

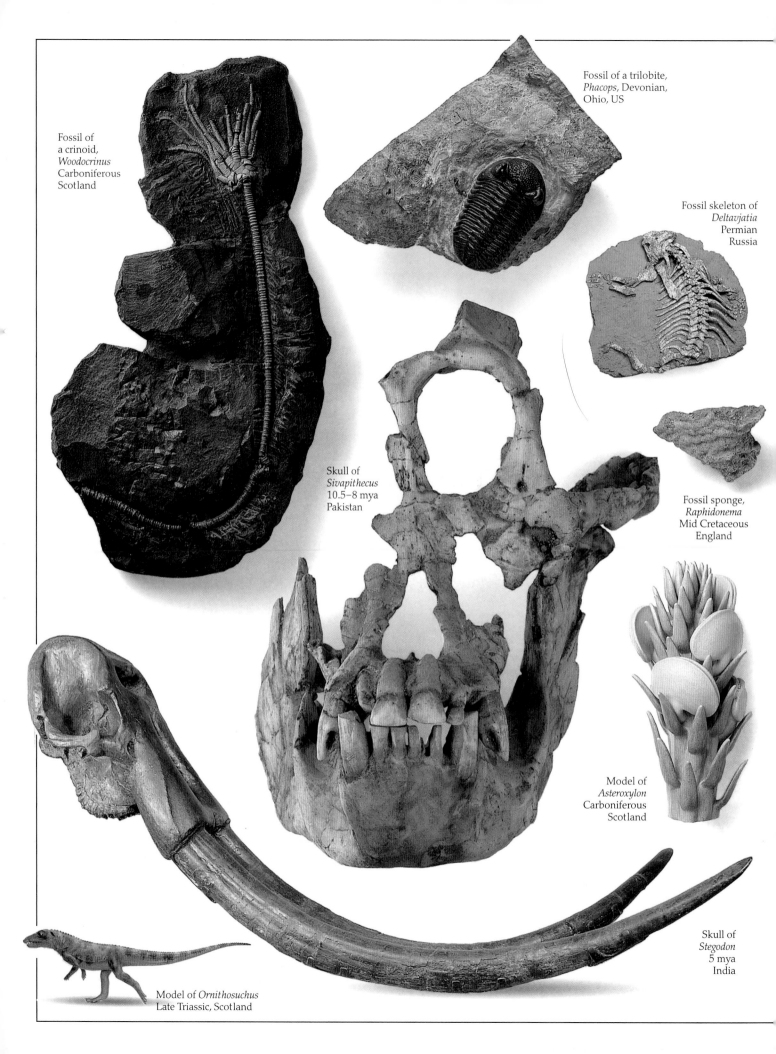

Fossil of a crinoid, *Woodocrinus* Carboniferous Scotland

Fossil of a trilobite, *Phacops*, Devonian, Ohio, US

Fossil skeleton of *Deltavjatia* Permian Russia

Fossil sponge, *Raphidonema* Mid Cretaceous England

Skull of *Sivapithecus* 10.5–8 mya Pakistan

Model of *Asteroxylon* Carboniferous Scotland

Skull of *Stegodon* 5 mya India

Model of *Ornithosuchus* Late Triassic, Scotland

Araucaria cone
Jurassic, Argentina

Model of
Homo habilis
Pliocene,
East Africa

Eyewitness
PREHISTORIC
LIFE

Written by
WILLIAM LINDSAY

Photographed by
HARRY TAYLOR

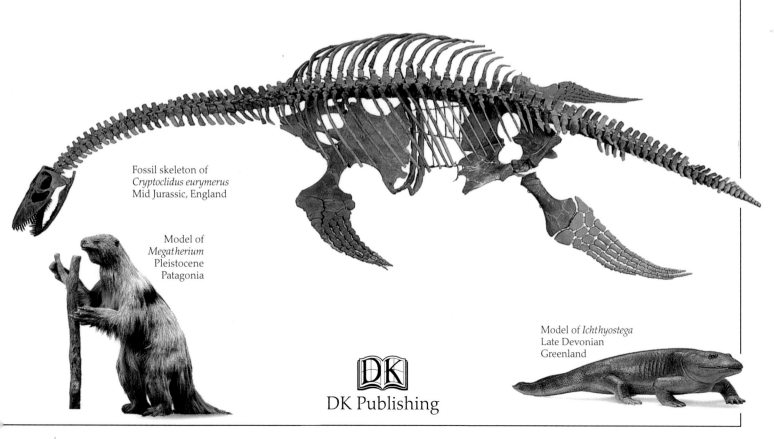

Fossil skeleton of
Cryptoclidus eurymerus
Mid Jurassic, England

Model of
Megatherium
Pleistocene
Patagonia

Model of *Ichthyostega*
Late Devonian
Greenland

DK Publishing

Model of
Arthropleura
Carboniferous
Scotland

LONDON, NEW YORK,
MELBOURNE, MUNICH, and DELHI

Project editor Marion Dent
Art editor Vicky Wharton
Managing editor Simon Adams
Managing art editor Julia Harris
Researcher Céline Carez
Picture researcher Deborah Pownall
Production Catherine Semark
Editorial consultant Dr. Robin Cocks, Head of
Palaeontology, Natural History Museum (London, England)
Special thanks to National Museums of Scotland
(Edinburgh), Hunterian Museum (University of Glasgow, Scotland),
Natural History Museum (London, England), Sedgwick and Zoology
Museums (University of Cambridge, England)

REVISED EDITION

Revised by Steve Brusatte

DK INDIA
Project editor Nidhi Sharma
Project art editor Rajnish Kashyap
Editor Shatarupa Chaudhuri
Designer Aanchal Awasthi
Deputy managing editor Eman Chowdhary
Managing art editor Romi Chakraborty
DTP designer Tarun Sharma
Picture researcher Sumedha Chopra

DK UK
Senior editor Rob Houston
Senior art editor Philip Letsu
Production editor Tony Phipps
Publisher Andrew Macintyre

First published in the United States in 1994
by DK Publishing, 375 Hudson Street, New York, New York 10014

12 11 10 9 8 7 6 5 4 3 2

002—183542—Jan/2012

DK books are available at special discounts when purchased in
bulk for sales promotions, premiums, fundraising, or educational use.
For details, contact: DK Publishing Special Markets
375 Hudson Street, New York, New York 10014
SpecialSales@dk.com

A catalog record for this book is available
from the Library of Congress.

ISBN: 978-0-7566-9077-9 (Hardback)
978-0-7566-9078-6 (Library binding)

Color reproduction by Colourscan, Singapore
Printed and bound in China
by Toppan Printing Co. (Shenzhen) Ltd.

Discover more at
www.dk.com

Fossil of *Archaeopteris*
Late Devonian, Ireland

Fossil skeleton of *Naso
rectifrons*, Late Eocene, Italy

Top view
of skull of
Simolestes
Mid Jurassic
England

Model of
Cothurnocystis
Late Ordovician
Scotland

Ediacara
Precambrian
Australia

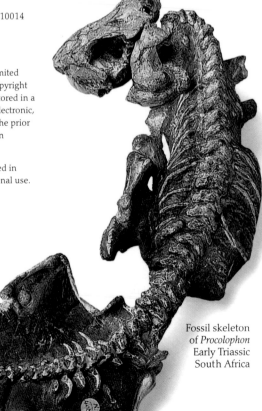

Fossil skeleton
of *Procolophon*
Early Triassic
South Africa

Contents

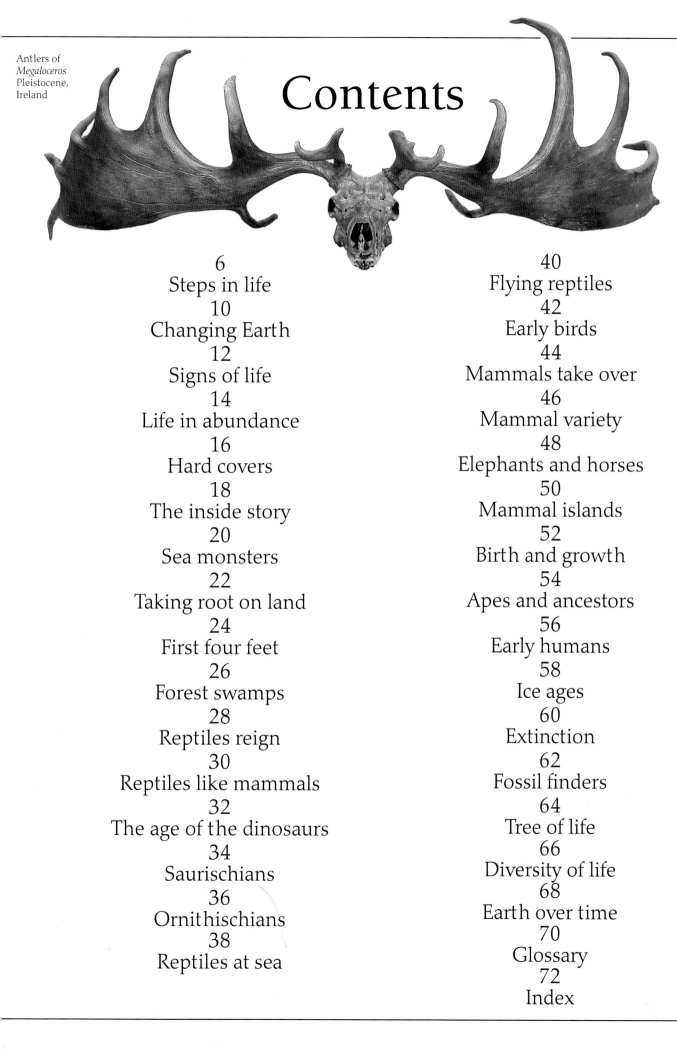

Antlers of *Megaloceros* Pleistocene, Ireland

Steps in life

How did life begin? No one knows for sure. Earth itself formed 4.5 billion years ago when clouds of particles drew together under great heat and pressure. Then, scientists believe, chemicals in the atmosphere combined up to 3.8 billion years ago and set off an explosion of life. Fossils—the hardened remains of dead plants and animals—show that different life forms evolved at different stages of Earth's geological history. At the bottom of the next few pages is a timeline of that history. It is divided into great eras lasting millions of years. Each era is divided into distinct periods or even shorter timespans called epochs.

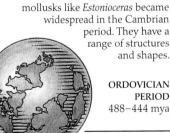
Cothurnocystis
Ordovician

SEABED DWELLER
Many animals build a supporting scaffold and protective shell for their bodies. Their shells were hard and are easily preserved as fossils. Seabed-dwelling *Cothurnocystis* (pp. 16–17), found in the UK, may be related to all backboned animals.

Metaldetes
Cambrian

CONE-SHAPED
Metaldetes was a spongelike marine animal (pp. 16–17). It had a double-walled skeleton to support its body.

CURIOUS FOSSIL
Jellyfish-like *Mawsonites* from Australia (pp. 12–13) is about 700 million years old. It may be one of the earliest multicelled animals.

Mawsonites
Precambrian, Australia

ROCKY MAT
Among the oldest, most primitive fossils, 3.4-billion-year-old stromatolites (pp. 12–13) were some of the first signs of life on Earth.

Collenia
(a stromatolite)
Precambrian, US

WEIRD ANIMAL
Whole communities of animals were fossilized together, as in Canada's Burgess Shale (pp. 14–15). Feather-shaped *Thaumaptilon* is from Burgess.

Estonioceras
Early Ordovician
Estonia

SPIRALS
Among the most common marine animals, mollusks like *Estonioceras* became widespread in the Cambrian period. They have a range of structures and shapes.

BUBBLING BEDS
Early Earth's surface was a hotbed of bubbling volcanoes and fiery lava flows (pp. 10–11). As Earth cooled, lavas hardened as rock.

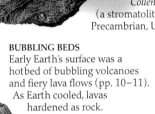

PRECAMBRIAN PERIOD
Before 542 mya (mya = millions of years ago)

CAMBRIAN PERIOD
542–488 mya

ORDOVICIAN PERIOD
488–444 mya

A SLOW START
The first part of geological history was the Precambrian, lasting some 4 billion years. Although very few rocks are left from the first billion years of the Precambrian, evidence suggests that early Earth had no oxygen in its air and no life on its land. The continents of today were probably joined as one or a few landmasses. The first simple life forms—single-celled bacteria and algae—evolved in the shallow primeval oceans of the Precambrian up to 3.8 billion years ago. Another billion years passed before an oxygen-rich atmosphere developed on Earth, and more complex, multicelled and soft-bodied organisms evolved.

HARD SHELLS
Cambrian animals developed body frames and shelly covers for protection. Trilobites (creatures with segmented armor) and brachiopods (clamlike, shelled animals) were common. There was one large landmass, Gondwanaland. North America, Europe, and Greenland existed as smaller, separate continents.

EARLY FISH
The first fishlike creatures developed. They had no backbones at first and no jaws. Worms, snails, and jellyfish became common. The Ordovician was a time of shrinking oceans and ice ages—periods when temperatures dropped and glaciers covered the land. Gondwanaland and the other continents were moving slowly together.

PRECAMBRIAN 4,600–570 mya   PALEOZOIC ERA 570–245 mya

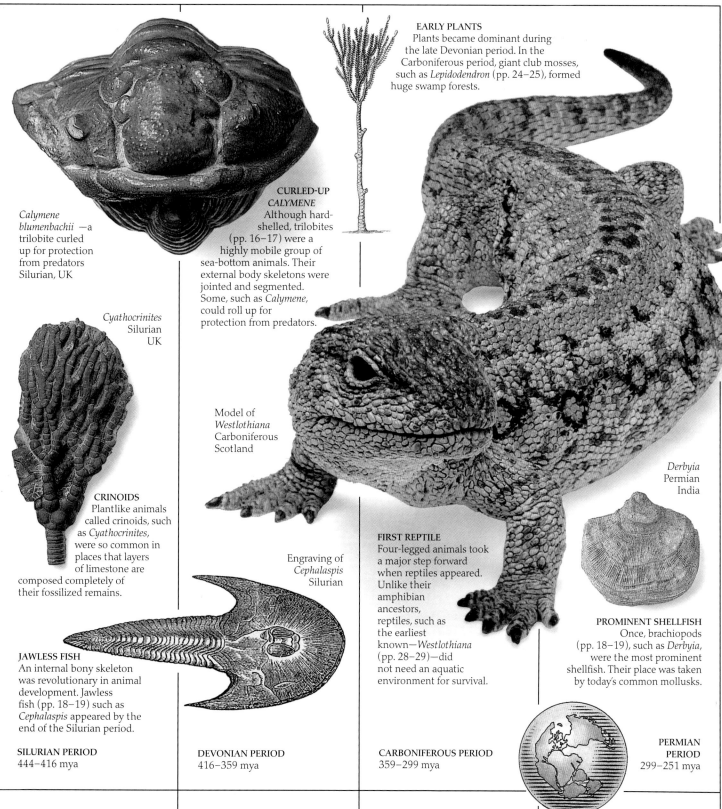

EARLY PLANTS
Plants became dominant during the late Devonian period. In the Carboniferous period, giant club mosses, such as *Lepidodendron* (pp. 24–25), formed huge swamp forests.

Calymene blumenbachii —a trilobite curled up for protection from predators Silurian, UK

CURLED-UP CALYMENE
Although hard-shelled, trilobites (pp. 16–17) were a highly mobile group of sea-bottom animals. Their external body skeletons were jointed and segmented. Some, such as *Calymene*, could roll up for protection from predators.

Cyathocrinites Silurian UK

Model of *Westlothiana* Carboniferous Scotland

Derbyia Permian India

CRINOIDS
Plantlike animals called crinoids, such as *Cyathocrinites*, were so common in places that layers of limestone are composed completely of their fossilized remains.

Engraving of *Cephalaspis* Silurian

FIRST REPTILE
Four-legged animals took a major step forward when reptiles appeared. Unlike their amphibian ancestors, reptiles, such as the earliest known—*Westlothiana* (pp. 28–29)—did not need an aquatic environment for survival.

PROMINENT SHELLFISH
Once, brachiopods (pp. 18–19), such as *Derbyia*, were the most prominent shellfish. Their place was taken by today's common mollusks.

JAWLESS FISH
An internal bony skeleton was revolutionary in animal development. Jawless fish (pp. 18–19) such as *Cephalaspis* appeared by the end of the Silurian period.

SILURIAN PERIOD
444–416 mya

DEVONIAN PERIOD
416–359 mya

CARBONIFEROUS PERIOD
359–299 mya

PERMIAN PERIOD
299–251 mya

INVASION OF LAND
Until the Silurian period, life on Earth had been confined to the oceans, with no organisms surviving out of water. During the Silurian, mountain ranges were forming across Scandinavia, Scotland, and the coast of North America. Plants made their first appearance on land, and giant scorpions hunted in the seas.

SWARMING SEAS
The invasion of land by animals continued in the Devonian period. While sharks and jawed fish became active predators in the seas, amphibians made their move onto land. As oceans narrowed, the giant continent of Gondwanaland closed in on Europe, North America, and Greenland.

THE FIRST REPTILES
During the Carboniferous period, the Earth's continents formed a single landmass, changing the environment for many forms of life. In the Northern Hemisphere, tropical climates produced vast, tree-filled swamps, preserved today as coal. Reptiles first appeared, able to lay eggs out of water.

MASS EXTINCTION
The continents fused together and moved as one landmass (Pangaea). Ice sheets covered South America, Antarctica, Australia, and Africa, locking up water and lowering the sea level. Dry, desert conditions existed in the north. The Permian period ended with mass extinctions on the largest scale ever.

Continued on next page

Continued from previous page

Model of
Megazostrodon
Late Triassic
South Africa

Life continues

After the mass extinctions at the end of the Permian 245 million years ago (mya), the Mesozoic era began, marked by huge geological changes and a wealth of new plant and animal life. Mammal-like reptiles became the most prominent animals. When they died out, dinosaurs appeared and dominated Earth. Mammals evolved and survived the extinction of the dinosaurs, as did the dinosaurs' descendants, the birds. Evolution took many twists and turns. Some paths led to the ancestors of today's animals—others led to dead ends: species only on Earth a short time before dying out.

FIRST FLYING MAMMALS
Palaeochiropteryx, a bat from Messel, Germany, looks very similar to today's bats.

FIRST BIRD
From among a group of small, two-legged, meat-eating dinosaurs came the first birds. About 150 mya, *Archaeopteryx* (pp. 42–43), still with reptile teeth, tail, and fingers, flew after its insect prey.

Engraving of
Archaeopteryx
Jurassic
Germany

SMALL MAMMALS
Megazostrodon developed from mammal-like reptiles near the end of the Triassic period. Unlike the cold-blooded reptiles, mammals maintained body heat with fur and with rapid processing of food for energy (pp. 44–51). Born live, mammal young fed on their mother's milk.

LONG TAIL
Leptictidium was an Eocene omnivore. Remains of plants, insects, and lizards have been found fossilized in its stomach area. The 8-in- (20-cm-) long tail acted as a counterbalance for its body during the chase.

Model of fearsome
Tyrannosaurus rex
Late Cretaceous
North America

LARGEST ANIMALS
Dinosaurs (pp. 32–37) lived on Earth for a long time, from the Triassic period to the end of the Cretaceous period, when they became extinct (pp. 60–61).

Reconstruction of *Leptictidium*
Eocene
Germany

Stenopterygius
Jurassic
Germany

TINY HORSE
Hyracotherium, the first known horse, appeared. It was only the size of a dog and ran on four-toed feet (pp. 48–49).

Hyracotherium
Late Paleocene to Early Eocene
North America and Europe

MARINE REPTILES
Not all reptiles were land based. Ichthyosaurs (pp. 38–39) made their home at sea. They did not lay eggs on land but gave birth (pp. 52–53) to live young at sea.

JURASSIC PERIOD
201.6 – 145.5 mya

CRETACEOUS PERIOD
145.5 – 65.5 mya

PALEOGENE PERIOD
65.5–23 mya

TRIASSIC PERIOD
251–201.6 mya

AGE OF REPTILES
Pangaea drifted northward. Deserts formed. Southern ice sheets melted, and cracks appeared in Pangaea. Many reptiles evolved on land, including dinosaurs, while others took to the air or lived in the sea.

REIGN OF THE DINOSAURS
Dinosaurs spread across the lands, ichthyosaurs hunted in the seas, and pterosaurs dominated in the air. Pangaea broke up as North America drifted away from Africa and South America from Antarctica and Australia.

DINOSAURS DIE OUT
Milder climates appeared. India drifted away from Africa toward Asia. Dinosaurs died out at the end of this period, along with many other species. The extinctions were possibly due to a comet or asteroid hitting Earth.

PALEOCENE EPOCH
65.5–55.8 mya
Mammals rapidly took over after the demise of the dinosaurs. Continents were now separate. Africa moved north on a collision course with Europe, while North America drifted eastward.

EOCENE EPOCH
55.8–33.9 mya
Swimming and flying mammals established many new habitats for themselves. India joined with Asia. The Atlantic Ocean separated Europe and North America. South America was on its own.

MESOZOIC ERA   245 mya – 65 mya

CENOZOIC ERA   65 mya – present

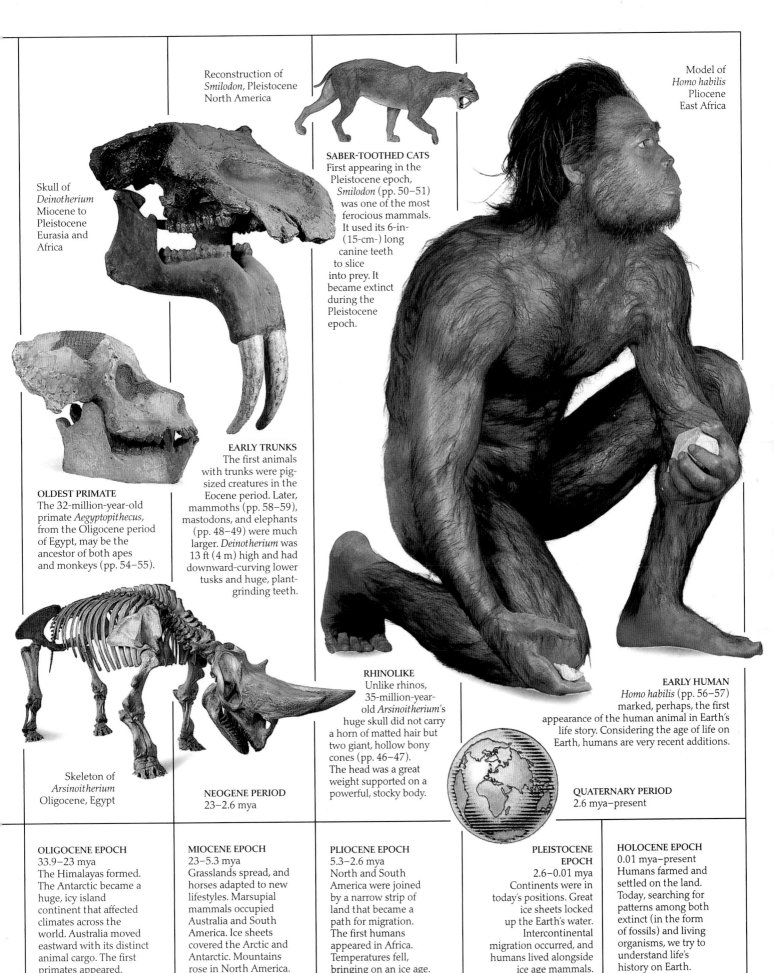

Reconstruction of *Smilodon*, Pleistocene North America

Model of *Homo habilis* Pliocene East Africa

Skull of *Deinotherium* Miocene to Pleistocene Eurasia and Africa

SABER-TOOTHED CATS
First appearing in the Pleistocene epoch, *Smilodon* (pp. 50–51) was one of the most ferocious mammals. It used its 6-in- (15-cm-) long canine teeth to slice into prey. It became extinct during the Pleistocene epoch.

OLDEST PRIMATE
The 32-million-year-old primate *Aegyptopithecus*, from the Oligocene period of Egypt, may be the ancestor of both apes and monkeys (pp. 54–55).

EARLY TRUNKS
The first animals with trunks were pig-sized creatures in the Eocene period. Later, mammoths (pp. 58–59), mastodons, and elephants (pp. 48–49) were much larger. *Deinotherium* was 13 ft (4 m) high and had downward-curving lower tusks and huge, plant-grinding teeth.

RHINOLIKE
Unlike rhinos, 35-million-year-old *Arsinoitherium's* huge skull did not carry a horn of matted hair but two giant, hollow bony cones (pp. 46–47). The head was a great weight supported on a powerful, stocky body.

EARLY HUMAN
Homo habilis (pp. 56–57) marked, perhaps, the first appearance of the human animal in Earth's life story. Considering the age of life on Earth, humans are very recent additions.

Skeleton of *Arsinoitherium* Oligocene, Egypt

NEOGENE PERIOD 23–2.6 mya

QUATERNARY PERIOD 2.6 mya–present

OLIGOCENE EPOCH 33.9–23 mya
The Himalayas formed. The Antarctic became a huge, icy island continent that affected climates across the world. Australia moved eastward with its distinct animal cargo. The first primates appeared.

MIOCENE EPOCH 23–5.3 mya
Grasslands spread, and horses adapted to new lifestyles. Marsupial mammals occupied Australia and South America. Ice sheets covered the Arctic and Antarctic. Mountains rose in North America.

PLIOCENE EPOCH 5.3–2.6 mya
North and South America were joined by a narrow strip of land that became a path for migration. The first humans appeared in Africa. Temperatures fell, bringing on an ice age.

PLEISTOCENE EPOCH 2.6–0.01 mya
Continents were in today's positions. Great ice sheets locked up the Earth's water. Intercontinental migration occurred, and humans lived alongside ice age mammals.

HOLOCENE EPOCH 0.01 mya–present
Humans farmed and settled on the land. Today, searching for patterns among both extinct (in the form of fossils) and living organisms, we try to understand life's history on Earth.

Changing Earth

FOR ALMOST A BILLION YEARS, nothing lived on Earth. Nothing wriggled, ran, flew or swam. That ancient, lifeless Earth was very different from the world today. But as the early planet was constantly evolving—as rocks formed, oceans spread, continents shifted, mountains rose, earthquakes and volcanoes shook and rattled the surface, and climates changed—the chance was created for life. The evidence of that life is today preserved as fossils found on the Earth's rocky surface.

HOT ROCKS
Volcanoes occur at weak, thin points in the Earth's crust. Molten lava pours out of cracks and solidifies as it cools. Ash and hot gases are thrown into the air, and the ash falls to form a volcanic cone. In the early stages of the Earth's formation, the world was a hot, molten mass.

Sedimentary sandstone is made of eroded quartz grains

Metamorphic marble was sedimentary limestone

Igneous granite solidified deep underground

Basalt is a common volcanic igneous rock

BUILDING BLOCKS
Igneous rocks form from molten rock material deep in the Earth and at the surface. Rock particles eroded by wind and water form sedimentary layers in rivers, seas, and lakes. Temperature and pressure can transform both igneous and sedimentary rocks into new, metamorphic rocks.

WATERY GRAVES
Rivers build thick sediment layers of sand and mud on flood plains and deltas. Reaching the sea, the sediment sinks to the seabed. Quickly buried, animal and plant remains may be preserved as sediments turn to rock.

The "part" of a trilobite

Volcanic ridge

Fault line

Plate-edge trench

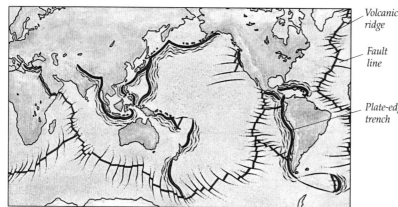

MOVING PLATES
Earth's surface is made of large, interlocking plates. New molten rock rises from volcanic ridges along the ocean floor and adds to the plates. As the plates grow and spread, their edges collide and sink into trenches, causing earthquakes and volcanoes. When continents carried on top of the plates collide, huge mountain ranges such as the Himalayas in Asia may be created.

FOSSIL EVIDENCE
Fossils are evidence of ancient life. They may preserve an organism's detailed inner structure as well as its outer shape. Flowers, feathers, and even footprints can be fossilized. Converting buried organisms into these stony replicas takes millions of years, as organic material is destroyed and minerals in the rocks slowly fill in microscopic spaces. Sometimes the buried fossil is destroyed completely in the rock, leaving a natural mold. The space left behind is filled with more rock material, producing a natural and accurate cast of the fossil's shape.

How a fossil is formed

Decaying (1) *Procolophon* was covered in silt, sediment swept in by shallow streams (2). Burial must have been rapid since the skeleton was not broken up, although the flesh rotted. Over millions of years, the skeleton was buried deep underground (3). Under pressure sands became stone, in which chemicals turned *Procolophon's* bones into fossil. Erosion brought the fossil back to the surface (4).

(1) Decaying and dead animal carcass lies exposed on Earth's surface

(2) Silt—sediments—from shallow streams quickly bury the body

(3) Sediments turn to rock around the fossil over millions of years

(4) Fossilized skeleton is exposed at the surface

"Counterpart" of a trilobite, *Flexicalymene caractaci* Ordovician, England

Procolophon trigoniceps Early Triassic South Africa

SMALL REPTILE

Procolophon was a small reptile that lived during the Early Triassic period. Its fossils are well known from South Africa's Karroo Basin. Complete skeletons and skulls, perfectly preserved as white fossil bone, are buried in a red, silty rock. This red color comes from iron minerals that hold the quartz grains together. It shows that the sediment was exposed to air and not continuously buried underwater, since iron rusts only in air.

HOT AND COLD

Rocks preserve clues of climatic conditions that help to explain the shifting continents. Fossils of the large-leaved *Glossopteris* are found in abundance in Antarctic Permian rocks. During this period, the Antarctic, part of a much larger continental mass, was not at the South Pole. Its climate was much warmer than it is today.

Fossil leaf

Glossopteris, Permian NSW, Australia

PART AND COUNTERPART

Splitting apart the rock reveals the positive "part" of the fossil and the negative "counterpart"—the natural mold. This trilobite's overall shape has been preserved, but the hard fossil skeleton was destroyed over many years. Fossils are often flattened by the pressure of overlying rock and may be cracked and broken into many pieces.

OLD AGE

Evidence from meteorites and moon rocks show that the Earth is 4.5 billion years old. The oldest rocks on Earth, about 4 billion years old, are found in northern Canada and are metamorphic. Some of these rocks were originally sediments, laid down at an even earlier stage.

Signs of life

ALTHOUGH LIFE MAY HAVE ORIGINATED earlier on Earth, microscopically small strands of single cells from 3.4–3.3-billion-year-old rocks in Australia and South Africa are among the oldest signs of life discovered. These are the remains of cyanobacteria (blue-green algae) that appeared a billion years after the Earth formed. Cyanobacteria are prokaryotes—simple, single-celled microorganisms. Many of them can live only in a low-oxygen environment. Plants, animals, and fungi are all eukaryotes; their cells are divided into separate compartments with each part having a special job to do. Eukaryotes first appeared about two billion years ago. They may have begun as a group of prokaryotes that joined together. Before this time, there was too little oxygen in the atmosphere for eukaryotes to survive and no ozone layer to protect them from the Sun's harmful ultraviolet light.

ALGAE MOUNDS
Mounds of stromatolites grow in the shallow, clear water of Shark Bay in Western Australia. Stromatolites are layers of intertwined blue-green algae that grow by photosynthesis, absorbing carbon dioxide and giving off oxygen.

Each layer shows a period of growth

GROWTH LINES
Mats of blue-green algae are sticky and trap sediment particles. Cemented together over the years, layers build up to make the lumpy mounds of rock that are found as fossilized stromatolites. Three-billion-year-old stromatolites have been found in South Africa.

Skakoper cryptozoan (a stromatolite) Proterozoic Minnesota, US

Scientists think Spriggina's *"head" was actually an attachment for a frond*

Dickinsonia *from Australia's Ediacara grew by adding new segments to its body*

An Ediacara *fossil, probably buried by sand where it lived during the Precambrian in South Australia*

Two jellyfish from Ediacara seem to have been fossilized side by side

SOFT IMPRESSIONS
In the Flinders Ranges of South Australia, quartz grains are cemented together in a hard, pinkish rock. The rock, about 700 million years old, may have formed in deep water during brief storms. In 1946, at Ediacara, fossils of some of the oldest known multicelled animals were discovered in these rocks. Impressions of delicate fronds, ridged disks, and segmented circles are all that are left of this mysterious group of soft-bodied animals. Segmented *Spriggina* might have been an annelid worm, a type of trilobite, or even an anchored frond. Other fossils might be jellyfish or even filled-in burrows of animals.

IN THE BEGINNING
The work of paleontologists is to find fossils and piece together the story of ancient life on Earth. But we also want to know how life began, and even the earliest fossils do not answer that question. In 1953, US chemist Stanley Miller showed how certain complex chemicals on which life depends—the building blocks of protein—could have first been produced on the Earth.

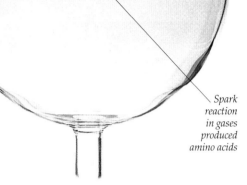

Powerful electric charge was fed into chamber

Spark reaction in gases produced amino acids

BRIGHT SPARK
Before blue-green algae produced oxygen-rich air, the Earth's atmosphere may have been an unhealthy mixture of gases, including methane, ammonia, hydrogen, and water vapor. Dr. Miller's experiment showed that these gases can be triggered by a powerful electric spark to produce amino acids. Amino acids are the chemicals that make protein molecules, which in turn are the main substance of living things.

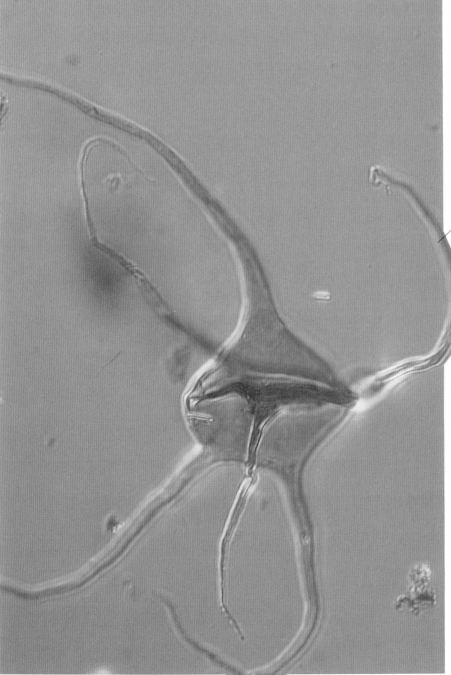

Spiny acritarch (Acanthomorph acritarch) extracted from Silurian rocks

An example of a carbonaceous chondrite meteorite, containing relatively high levels of carbon

METEORITE MOLECULES
Evidence that the molecules needed for life can form naturally comes from outer space. One meteorite, of a type called carbonaceous chondrites, fell near Murchison, Australia, in 1969. Scientists who studied it discovered amino acids just like those made artificially in Dr. Miller's experiments.

CONFUSED REMAINS
Understanding fossil life can be difficult. Sometimes this is reflected in the names given to fossils. Crushed and flattened, spiky or smooth, a group of microscopic spheres, ellipsoids, and three-sided pouches that first appeared about 1,800 million years ago are known as acritarchs, from the Greek for "of uncertain origin." They are some of the earliest-known eukaryotes and were seagoing microalgae.

Life in abundance

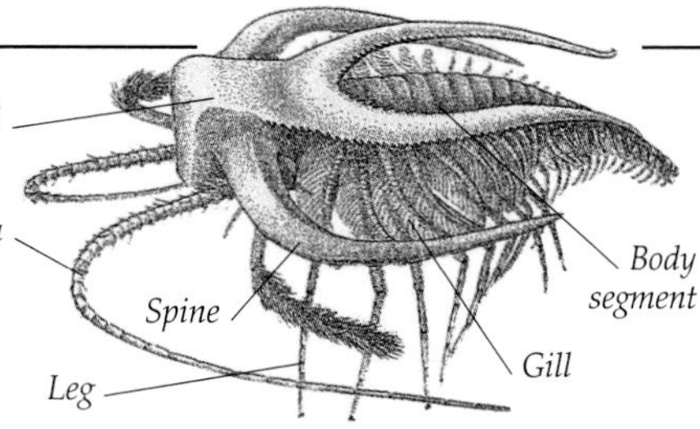

MARRELLA
Delicate and segmented *Marrella* fed by sieving food particles from the mud as its pairs of jointed legs carried it over the surface of the seabed. Paired feathery gills took in oxygen from the water.

Labels: Head shield, Antenna, Spine, Leg, Gill, Body segment

FOLLOWING THE STORY OF LIFE on earth is rarely simple. Many animals have left no trace and the fossil record is far from complete. In the book of life, it is difficult to make sense of what is happening on one page when the pages on either side are missing. The fossils of the 505-million-year-old Burgess Shale in Canada's Rocky Mountains show that life was already very diverse and major groups were already present. After more than 100 million years of blank spaces, the silvery traces preserved in thin sections of slate appear without much warning. Here, 8,000 ft (2400 m) above sea level, a slaty rock layer contains an incredible catalog of soft-bodied and thin-shelled sea animals, very different from the creatures that left their mark at Ediacara (pp. 12–13) long before. Although many Burgess Shale fossils are similar to today's living animals, others have a unique body shape seen nowhere else before or since. It seems that 505 million years ago, life may have been even more varied than today.

Labels: Antenna, Head shield, Body segment

Rockies' guide Tom Wilson

Prof. Walcott

MARVELOUS MULTITUDE
Marrella is the most common animal fossilized in the Burgess Shale—more than 13,000 specimens have now been collected. Up to 0.75 in (2 cm) long, *Marrella* had a head shield from which two pairs of spines swept back over its body. The body had 24 to 26 segments, and each segment was biramous (two-branched). The upper branch had long gills; the lower had a walking leg. Fossils of *Marrella* show the exceptional preservation of detail among the Burgess Shale animals. Swept up in an underwater landslip and quickly buried, the bodies were sealed before they could rot and fall apart.

DISCOVERER
Professor Charles D. Walcott (1850–1927), Secretary of the Smithsonian Institution in Washington, D.C., discovered the Burgess Shale treasure in 1909. Over six field seasons, Walcott collected 65,000 specimens, but it is only in recent decades that paleontologists have come to appreciate the novelty of these fossils, which are mostly in the collections of the Smithsonian and the Geological Survey of Canada in Ottawa.

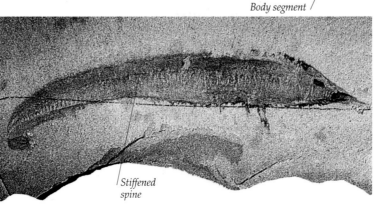

Stiffened spine

ODD ONE OUT
Among all the invertebrates (animals without backbones) from the Burgess Shale, such as worms, echinoderms, sponges, and arthropods, 1.5-in- (4-cm-) long *Pikaia* is the odd one out. It looks like a fish, but Walcott identified it as an annelid (segmented worm). Scientists now believe the ghostly *Pikaia* may be the first-known chordate (an early vertebrate) and a forerunner of the vertebrate group that includes humans.

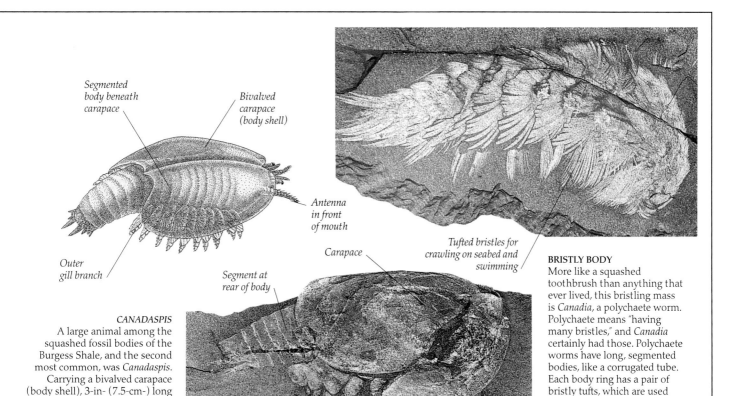

Segmented
body beneath
carapace

Bivalved
carapace
(body shell)

Antenna
in front
of mouth

Outer
gill branch

Carapace

Segment at
rear of body

Tufted bristles for
crawling on seabed and
swimming

Gill   Leg

BRISTLY BODY
More like a squashed
toothbrush than anything that
ever lived, this bristling mass
is *Canadia*, a polychaete worm.
Polychaete means "having
many bristles," and *Canadia*
certainly had those. Polychaete
worms have long, segmented
bodies, like a corrugated tube.
Each body ring has a pair of
bristly tufts, which are used
for crawling and swimming.
Living polychaetes include the
ragworm, which burrows in
muddy seashores.

CANADASPIS
A large animal among the
squashed fossil bodies of the
Burgess Shale, and the second
most common, was *Canadaspis*.
Carrying a bivalved carapace
(body shell), 3-in- (7.5-cm-) long
Canadaspis has been shown to be
a distant relative of shrimps,
prawns, and lobsters. Underneath
the shell was a head with eyes, a
body of 15 segments, and 10
pairs of legs and gills.

Head

Spine

Stiff spine

Head

Anal tube for
getting rid of
waste products

Leg for walking
on seabed

WHICH WAY UP?
New discoveries in China of fossils of
Hallucigenia as old as those from the
Burgess Shale suggest that the original
scientific reconstruction of this animal
was upside down, but the correct version
is shown here. Seven pairs of stilts and
long feeding tentacles turned out to be
back spines and walking legs.

BAD DREAMS
Perhaps the most curious of all the
creatures that lived on the Burgess
seabed was the stilted 1-in (2.5-cm)
Hallucigenia. What kind of animal
has seven pairs of spines, seven
tentacles, and a tube-shaped body
with a narrower tube at one end and
a balloon at the other? *Hallucigenia*
was so bizarre that scientists could
not be sure which end was which
or even which way was up! New
discoveries in China have identified
Hallucigenia as a caterpillar-shaped
velvet worm. Another gap in the
fossil record has been filled.

Leg

Anal
tube

Spine

Ridged scale
overlapping
with its
neighbor

Oval-shaped
Wiwaxia

A FEATHERED CAP
Scales and spines are almost all there
is to see of oval-shaped, 1.5-in (4-cm)
Wiwaxia, an animal almost unknown
anywhere but at Burgess Shale, but
perhaps distantly related to mollusks.
The ridged, flattened scales overlap,
making a scaly cap. The spines stand
up in two rows to defend the animal. A
pair of tiny toothed bars were used for
feeding. One other piece of evidence
gives a fuller picture of *Wiwaxia*. Fossil
brachiopods, attached to some scales,
tell us that whatever *Wiwaxia* was, it
crawled along the muddy seabed and
not under it, where brachiopods
would not have survived.

Hard covers

Model of *Cothurnocystis elizae*

Small slit for getting rid of waste water

"Tail" (stem) for moving over sea floor

IN THE 200 MILLION YEARS between the creatures of Ediacara (pp. 12–13) and the diverse life of the Burgess Shale (pp. 14–15), life under the sea took a great evolutionary advance. Soft-bodied creatures evolved into animals with hard shells. Calcite (the calcium carbonate mineral in chalk and limestone) was one of the main materials for building shells. Animals grew calcite, forming a complete stony covering or patchwork of plates. Wraparound shells transformed life in the oceans. Trilobites, free to swim or to crawl over the seabed, flexed their exoskeletons (external skeletons) with internal muscles. In their fortress homes cemented to rocks, corals and brachiopods could grow and feed. Shells and exoskeletons let animals create their own living environments, safe from predators. Thanks to these hard bodies, millions of fascinating fossils are preserved in rocks all over the world.

Dactylioceras commune
Early Jurassic
UK

CARVED HEAD
In the Middle Ages, ammonites—fossil shells— were thought to be snakes turned to stone; snakes' heads were carved on them.

Mouth at open end of "boot"

Boot-shaped head

ANIMAL ANCESTOR?
Like an odd-shaped fork, and small enough to hold in your hand, *Cothurnocystis elizae* (440 mya) was a strange but important animal. Some scientists believe that its ancestors were also the ancestors of all animals with backbones, including humans. Covered in hard, calcite plates, the boot-shaped head was pulled across the mud by its long stem. Water was drawn in the open end of the "boot" and filtered for food before being pushed out of the slits around the "toe."

Slit at "toe" end

Cothurnocystis elizae
Late Ordovician
Scotland

Tiny tube extended from plated arm to catch food

Crystalline plate covering body

Calcite rings form a flexible stem

SEA LILY
Sometimes called sea lilies, crinoids such as this *Woodocrinus* were anchored in seabed gardens by long, jointed stems of calcite. Above the seabed, food was caught by sticky tubes along the jointed waving arms and carried via grooves to a mouth on the plated cup. Crinoids, some of which still live today, first appeared about 500 mya. Although they look like plants, crinoids are close relatives of sea urchins and starfish.

Raphidonema faringdonense (sponge)
Mid Cretaceous
England

SPIKY SPONGES
Soft and luxurious, many sponges actually have a basketwork skeleton of tiny struts and spikes. This vase-shaped sponge skeleton is made of calcite. Others are made of silica, the same hard mineral that makes glass. These skeletons formed a cagelike framework that held the sponge body together and anchored it to the seabed.

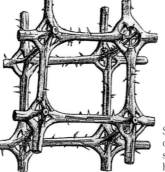

Skeleton of a sponge, showing its hard, sharp structure

Woodocrinus liddesdalensis
Carboniferous
Scotland

PROTECTIVE OVERCOAT
Trilobites dominated the earliest sea world of hard cases and survived until about 245 mya. Unlike bivalves and corals, which grow larger by adding material around the rims of their shells, trilobites had to cast off their "straitjackets." Exposed and in danger, their bodies grew and produced a new, larger cover to regain protection. This process happened several times. Many trilobites' castoffs were fossilized, giving a false idea of trilobite numbers.

Large eye was composed of many lenses

Phacops africanus
Devonian
Western Sahara

Large, curved eye gave excellent all-around vision

Head (cephalon) concealed mouth and stomach

Line of weakness in trilobite's skeleton allowed it to be discarded for a new, larger skeleton

When trilobite rolled up body for safety, each body segment hinged with its neighbor

Tail locked into groove under head for protection

Opening where tough stalk anchored brachiopod to seabed

FEEDING SHELLS
At first glance, brachiopods seem indistinguishable from the many bivalved seashells found today. In fact, they belong to a very different animal group, which first appeared in the Early Cambrian. Brachiopods grow by adding crystals and organic material from the outer edges of the body to the surrounding edges of the shell. When the shell is open, tiny waving threads on the sticky lophophore (a ring of tentacles) draw in water while the lophophore filters food from the sea.

Hinge opened and closed both parts of shell

Spirifer
Carboniferous
Ireland

Body segment

Tail is a single plate of fused segments

Phacops rana
Devonian
Ohio, US

EMPIRE BUILDING
Fantastically shaped coral reefs are rich in sea life. In a modern coral reef, hard, multistoried colonies of living coral build on top of cemented coral skeletons. The earliest-known reefs were made by algae about 2 bya, but corals did not join the reef builders until the middle of the Ordovician period, about 470 mya. Today's coral reefs grow in shallow waters at temperatures above 64°F (18°C).

THE FIRST EYE
Trilobites were the first creatures to see. Their excellent vision detected movement and size in low levels of light in the water. Like other sea creatures with hard covers, they extracted from digested food and seawater the minerals needed for their shells. After death, the shells became part of the sediment on the seabed. Fossil trilobites, with pairs of legs under the head, tail, and body segments, are often preserved without any trace of their delicate antennae or legs. Beside each leg was a feathery breathing gill, which may also have aided in swimming. Body segments were grown one at a time until the full adult number was reached.

Cup where polyp sat when it was alive

Ketophyllum
Silurian
Sweden

CORAL LIFE
This many-branched fossil coral was once a colony of fleshy animals. A soft-bodied coral animal (polyp) sat in each hollow cup at the end of a branch. Feathery tentacles ringed its upward-facing mouth, swaying in the water currents. As the polyp grew, it added more calcium carbonate to the skeleton beneath, increasing the height and width of its stony tower. Deep folds in the animal's underside helped form radiating ribs that supported the growing coral structure.

The inside story

FROZEN FISH
Louis Agassiz (1807–73), the Swiss-American naturalist, was a great student of fish, and the discoverer of the movement of glaciers.

Wітнін 60 мільйон years of Burgess Shale life, one group of animals, the vertebrates, escaped the restrictions of living in shells. They developed an internal bony skeleton that anchored muscles and supported internal organs. Bones are made of hard mineral crystals plus fibrous protein. Cells inside bones are fed by blood vessels, keeping the bones nourished. Bones, teeth, and scales are tough and preserve well as fossils. The first vertebrates were jawless fish, which probably evolved more than 500 million years ago. Some, like cephalaspids and placoderms, carried a heavy outer armor that restricted them to living on seabeds. Later fish types had less bony covering on their heads and had toothed, gaping jaws. The success of advanced, mobile bony fish (the teleosts) is seen in the vast numbers living today in rivers, lakes, and seas.

Head

Tail

MYSTERIOUS TEETH
For over 100 years, scientists debated whether the tiny, toothlike spikes of conodonts were remains of mollusks, fish, worms, or plants. The mystery was solved in Scotland when a set of Early Carboniferous conodont fossils were found in the fossilized remains of a long, soft, eel-like body—possibly a primitive swimming chordate (early vertebrate).

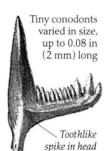

Tiny conodonts varied in size, up to 0.08 in (2 mm) long

Toothlike spike in head

HEAVY ARMOR
One of the most armored of placoderm fishes was the 370-million-year-old, 5-in (13-cm) *Pterichthyodes*. It had no inner bone skeleton. A shell of bony plates covered both the head and body. Even the pectoral fins were enclosed in a bony casing and would not have been of much use for swimming.

Spiny pectoral fin used for punting along the muddy sea bottom

Pterichthyodes milleri
Middle Devonian
Scotland

Homocercal (symmetrical) two-part caudal (tail) fin

Birkenia elegans
Silurian, Scotland

Dorsal spine

Lepidotes elvensis
Early Jurassic
Germany

SMALL SCALE
Distinctive 3-in- (7-cm-) long *Birkenia*, with its heterocercal (unequally divided), down-turned tail, was a freshwater jawless fish that lived about 425 mya. Overlapping bony scales covered the body, and several hooked spines protruded from the dorsal (top) surface. Small plates formed a mosaic on top of the head, while gill openings formed a diagonal dotted line behind.

SENSITIVE SUCKER
The first fishes were jawless, sucking food and water through their mouths. *Cephalaspis* had a bony shield covering its jawless head, as well as a pair of pectoral fins protected by swept-back spines. Two eyes and a single nostril perched on the crest of the arched head shield, which had three sensitive, scale-covered patches connected to the brain. *Cephalaspis* and *Birkenia* were ostracoderms, fishes with "bony skins."

Cephalaspis pagei
Devonian, Scotland

Eye

OLD STORY

The absence from some rocks of a particular fossil may mean that the animal was never fossilized or that it had already become extinct. For years, paleontologists believed that all coelacanths had died out 65 mya at the end of the Cretaceous period. Then a live coelacant was caught in 1938 off the east coast of South Africa. Since that time, other coelacanths have been found by fishermen off the coast of Madagascar. Along with lungfish (pp. 24–25), coelacanths, such as 14-in- (36-cm-) long *Holophagus*, are sarcopterygians (lobe-finned bony fish).

Lobed tail

Fleshy, lobed pectoral fin made up of large rays

Holophagus penicillata Late Jurassic, Germany

Eye

LIVING COELACANTH

Latimeria, the only known living coelacanth, is one of only seven species of lobe-finned fish found today.

Trilobed tail

Anal fin

Flexible vertebral column

Upturned, toothed jaw

HERRING BONE

Diplomystus, from the Green River Shale, Wyoming, shows the bony skeleton of bony fish. Unlike *Lepidotes*, the scales are reduced in size and thickness. The skeleton was very flexible, allowing an efficient swimming action. At a length of 17 in (43 cm), *Diplomystus* was a large-sized member of the group of fishes that includes the herring, sardine, and anchovy. Like most living actinopterygians (ray-finned fish), it is a teleost.

Homocercal, two-part caudal fin

Diplomystus dentatus, Eocene, Wyoming, US

Dorsal fin supported on ray of fine bones

Large eye socket

Wide gaping mouth caused by many joints in face and jaw bones

Gill cover

Pectoral fin

RAY FINS

Beautifully preserved in its heavy coat of shiny scales, 4-ft- (1.2-m-) long *Lepidotes* must have been a stiff swimmer. Like most living fish, it belonged to the large group of bony fish known as actinopterygians. Their trademark is fins supported by rays of bones. Such fins, along with a gas-filled swim bladder (or air bladder) that aids buoyancy, give the ray-finned fish control of their position in the water. *Lepidotes* used its crushing teeth on shelly, bottom-dwelling invertebrates.

PERFECT ANGEL

Perfectly preserved, this 4.75-in- (12-cm-) long skeleton needs only a little color to match the brightly patterned angelfish that swim among today's coral reefs. From Monte Bolca, a famous fossil locality in northern Italy, *Naso rectifrons* picked small prey from crevices, deterring predators with its startling colors.

Angelfish

Naso rectifrons Late Eocene Italy

Sea monsters

Tales of sea monsters have been told since people first set out to explore the world's great oceans and lakes. These myths still exist, from mermaids and Moby Dick, the legendary whale, to Scotland's Loch Ness monster. In the history of the world's seas, there has been no shortage of monstrous creatures. Many of the early forms of life were confined to living on the seabed. Others actively hunted their neighbors where, in this competitive world, larger size was one good means of survival. Giant predators have appeared in many groups of animals. Among arthropods, the scorpion-like eurypterid, *Pterygotus*, reached the monstrous size of 7 ft (2 m) and hunted fish. Many other enormous fishes emerged, such as *Dunkleosteus* and later *Xiphactinus*, but it was the emergence of biting jaws among the fishes that helped them dominate other life forms in the seas, lakes, and rivers. Even the rise of ferocious marine reptiles (pp. 38–39) failed to overcome the continued success of fish.

SILURIAN SEASCAPE
Predatory eurypterids (aquatic, scorpion-like arthropods) dominated life in the sea during the Silurian period (439–408 mya). While most fishes were still without jaws and scouring the seabed for food, eurypterids were among the most active hunters. Some later specimens were 7 ft (2 m) long.

Row of teeth rimmed bulldog-shaped jaw

WHAT A CATCH!
Of today's 21,700 fish species, almost 20,000 are teleosts (bony fish). No living bony fish surpasses *Xiphactinus* in size. When alive, this 13-ft-9-in- (4.2-m-) long specimen may have weighed as much as 1,650 lb (750 kg). *Xiphactinus* lived about 80 mya in the Cretaceous seas of Europe, Australia, and North America. The large, conical teeth along the margins of its jaws were probably the last things its captured prey ever saw.

Operculum (gill cover)

Pectoral fin

Jointed last leg with oar-shaped paddle

Eurypterus lacustris
Silurian, New York, US

Small chelicera (jointed pincer)

PINCERS AND PADDLES
A distant relative of today's scorpions and spiders, eurypterids first appeared about 470 mya. They had the segmented body typical of arthropods, such as trilobites (pp. 16–17), and were equipped with two chelicerae (jointed pincers) for biting prey. This eurypterid specimen (shown from the underside) had six pairs of appendages: the pair of pincers in front of the mouth for catching food, four pairs of jointed legs for walking on the seabed, and a pair of flat-ended paddles for swimming in the sea.

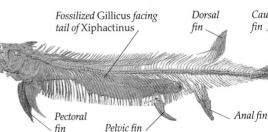

Fossilized Gillicus *facing tail of* Xiphactinus

Dorsal fin

Caudal fin

Pectoral fin

Pelvic fin

Anal fin

FISH FOOD
Paleontologists have no difficulty in finding out what *Xiphactinus* preyed on in the Cretaceous sea. Several complete fossil skeletons have been discovered with the complete fossil of another fish, *Gillicus*, lying inside the rib cage. *Gillicus* was no small fry itself, at 6 ft (1.8 m) long. Some scientists have suggested that these "stuffed" *Xiphactinus* died of gluttony, unable to digest the whole fish they had swallowed!

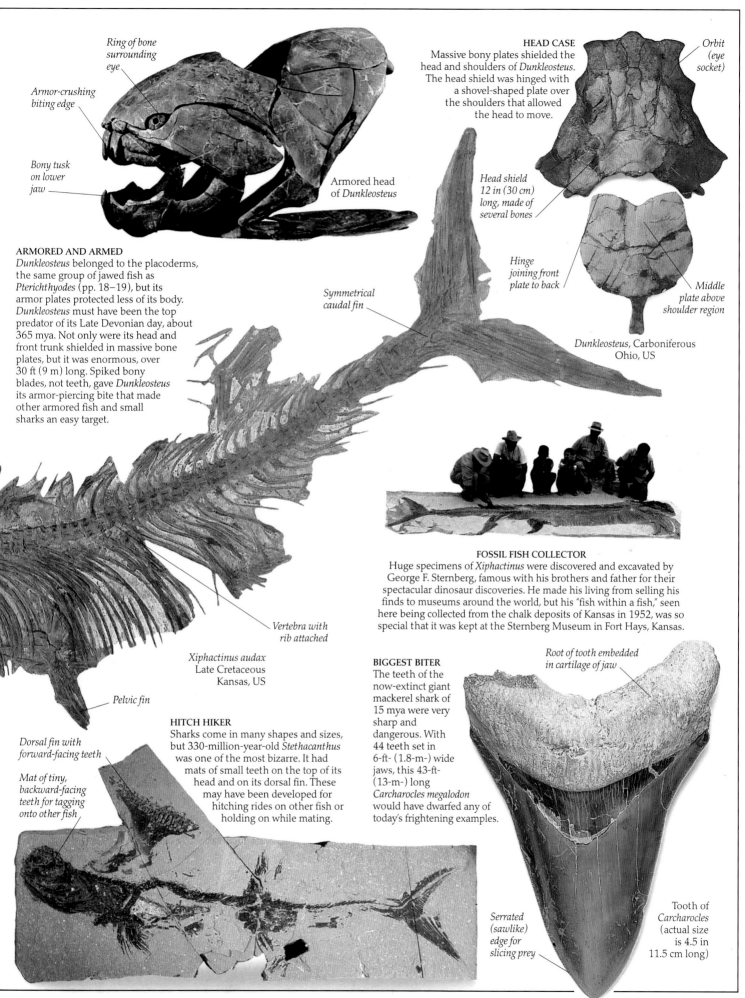

Ring of bone surrounding eye

Armor-crushing biting edge

Bony tusk on lower jaw

Armored head of *Dunkleosteus*

HEAD CASE
Massive bony plates shielded the head and shoulders of *Dunkleosteus*. The head shield was hinged with a shovel-shaped plate over the shoulders that allowed the head to move.

Orbit (eye socket)

Head shield 12 in (30 cm) long, made of several bones

Hinge joining front plate to back

Middle plate above shoulder region

Dunkleosteus, Carboniferous Ohio, US

ARMORED AND ARMED
Dunkleosteus belonged to the placoderms, the same group of jawed fish as *Pterichthyodes* (pp. 18–19), but its armor plates protected less of its body. *Dunkleosteus* must have been the top predator of its Late Devonian day, about 365 mya. Not only were its head and front trunk shielded in massive bone plates, but it was enormous, over 30 ft (9 m) long. Spiked bony blades, not teeth, gave *Dunkleosteus* its armor-piercing bite that made other armored fish and small sharks an easy target.

Symmetrical caudal fin

FOSSIL FISH COLLECTOR
Huge specimens of *Xiphactinus* were discovered and excavated by George F. Sternberg, famous with his brothers and father for their spectacular dinosaur discoveries. He made his living from selling his finds to museums around the world, but his "fish within a fish," seen here being collected from the chalk deposits of Kansas in 1952, was so special that it was kept at the Sternberg Museum in Fort Hays, Kansas.

Vertebra with rib attached

Xiphactinus audax
Late Cretaceous
Kansas, US

Pelvic fin

BIGGEST BITER
The teeth of the now-extinct giant mackerel shark of 15 mya were very sharp and dangerous. With 44 teeth set in 6-ft- (1.8-m-) wide jaws, this 43-ft- (13-m-) long *Carcharocles megalodon* would have dwarfed any of today's frightening examples.

Root of tooth embedded in cartilage of jaw

Dorsal fin with forward-facing teeth

Mat of tiny, backward-facing teeth for tagging onto other fish

HITCH HIKER
Sharks come in many shapes and sizes, but 330-million-year-old *Stethacanthus* was one of the most bizarre. It had mats of small teeth on the top of its head and on its dorsal fin. These may have been developed for hitching rides on other fish or holding on while mating.

Serrated (sawlike) edge for slicing prey

Tooth of *Carcharocles* (actual size is 4.5 in 11.5 cm long)

21

Taking root on land

LIVING IN WATER HAS ADVANTAGES. There is no risk of drying out, and food streams by. Organisms do not even have to support their full weight—the water does it for them. When plants moved out of water and onto dry land, they needed new ways to survive. The earliest-known evidence for land plants—spores and not leaves—comes from the Middle Ordovician about 470 million years ago. *Cooksonia*, one of the oldest land plants, lived about 430 million years ago. Corrugated tubes of long cells (tracheid tubes) kept plants upright and also provided a system of channels for carrying water up the stem. Roots absorbed water from the soil. These new "vascular" plants developed a cuticle, a waterproof coating to keep moisture in, with pores that allowed plants to "breathe." Wherever plants appeared, arthropods followed. Plants offered them a food supply and a new habitat.

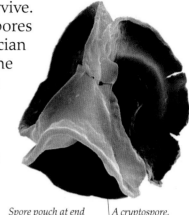

Spore pouch at end of Cooksonia's stem | *A cryptospore, Tetrahedraletes*

SILURIAN GREENERY
Vascular plants appeared near the end of the Silurian period. Many of these plants were small, like *Cooksonia*. Some lived in damp, swampy habitats where green algae were already present. Arthropods browsed through dead vegetation, processing it and improving the quality of the soil.

Sporangium at end of single stem of modern liverwort

Single sporangium on tip of stem

Disk-shaped sporangium on side of stem

Leaflike scale of Asteroxylon

Early reconstruction of Aglaophyton's simple root system with three-layered stems

EARLY PLANTS
Primitive land plants reproduced by releasing spores into the wind. *Cooksonia* (like the modern liverwort) carried spores in 0.04-in- (1-mm-) diameter pouches (sporangia) on the end of flattened, branching stems. Cryptospores, such as *Tetrahedraletes*, are known from the Devonian period and may belong to the family of bryophytes, plants that do not have a vascular system that carries water.

Modern springtail similar to the first-known insect, *Rhyniella*, found at Rhynie

Protacarus, a predatory mite from Rhynie (Devonian period)

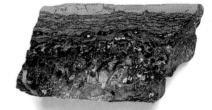

Fossilized plants are contained in this piece of Rhynie Chert, a silica-rich rock from Scotland

Hot waters

Rhynie plants were preserved by silica-rich water from volcanic hot springs. A thick gel of silica (a quartzlike mineral) preserved the plants and many stems, spores, and leaves. Even the remains of spiders, mites, and other arthropods have been preserved. *Asteroxylon*, 20-in (50-cm) tall, carried large, flat spore pouches (sporangia) among its scaly leaves. *Aglaophyton major* had 7-in (18-cm), smooth stems and combined features of bryophytes and vascular plants.

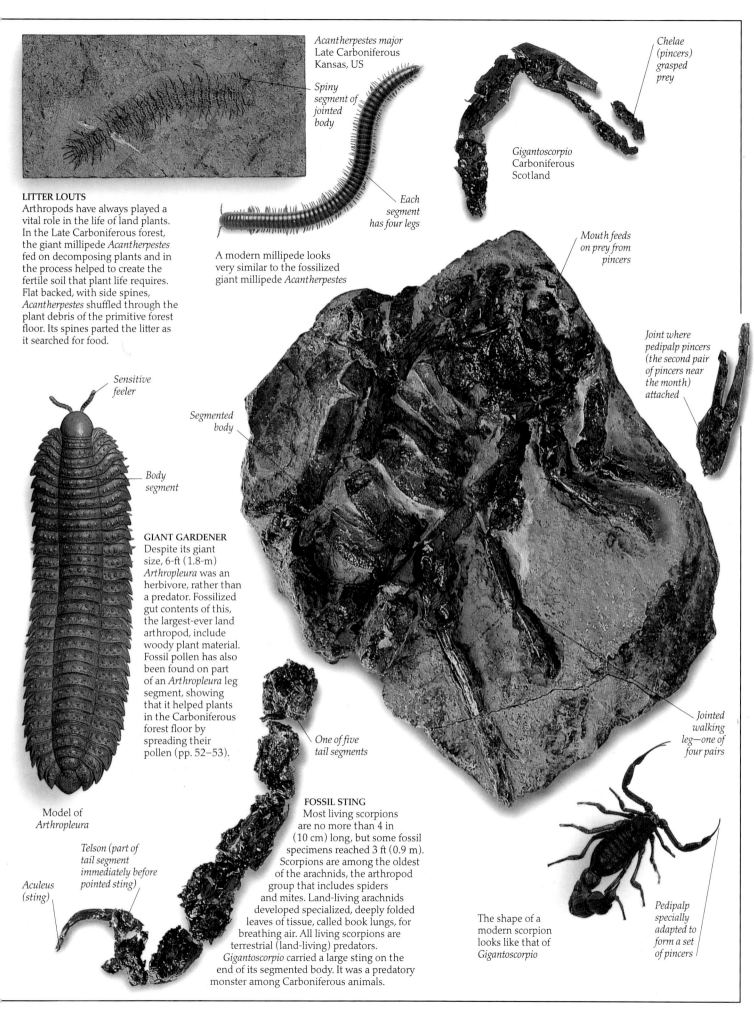

Acantherpestes major
Late Carboniferous
Kansas, US

Spiny segment of jointed body

Chelae (pincers) grasped prey

LITTER LOUTS
Arthropods have always played a vital role in the life of land plants. In the Late Carboniferous forest, the giant millipede *Acantherpestes* fed on decomposing plants and in the process helped to create the fertile soil that plant life requires. Flat backed, with side spines, *Acantherpestes* shuffled through the plant debris of the primitive forest floor. Its spines parted the litter as it searched for food.

Gigantoscorpio
Carboniferous
Scotland

Each segment has four legs

A modern millipede looks very similar to the fossilized giant millipede *Acantherpestes*

Mouth feeds on prey from pincers

Sensitive feeler

Segmented body

Joint where pedipalp pincers (the second pair of pincers near the month) attached

Body segment

GIANT GARDENER
Despite its giant size, 6-ft (1.8-m) *Arthropleura* was an herbivore, rather than a predator. Fossilized gut contents of this, the largest-ever land arthropod, include woody plant material. Fossil pollen has also been found on part of an *Arthropleura* leg segment, showing that it helped plants in the Carboniferous forest floor by spreading their pollen (pp. 52–53).

One of five tail segments

Jointed walking leg—one of four pairs

Model of
Arthropleura

Telson (part of tail segment immediately before pointed sting)

Aculeus (sting)

FOSSIL STING
Most living scorpions are no more than 4 in (10 cm) long, but some fossil specimens reached 3 ft (0.9 m). Scorpions are among the oldest of the arachnids, the arthropod group that includes spiders and mites. Land-living arachnids developed specialized, deeply folded leaves of tissue, called book lungs, for breathing air. All living scorpions are terrestrial (land-living) predators. *Gigantoscorpio* carried a large sting on the end of its segmented body. It was a predatory monster among Carboniferous animals.

The shape of a modern scorpion looks like that of *Gigantoscorpio*

Pedipalp specially adapted to form a set of pincers

First four feet

STEPPING FROM THEIR WATERY HABITAT onto dry land, the earliest amphibians had many fishlike features, including a wide, fishy tail. Clumsy in appearance, with short, squat limbs, these first tetrapods—four-footed animals with digits (fingers and toes)—had no competition in their new land life. In water, their ancestors had been just "small fish" in a big pool, but on land tetrapods entered a new world. To live on land, tetrapods had to be able to breathe air and have a skeleton and muscles strong enough to support their weight out of water. The newest evidence shows that legs, which seem essential on dry land, were developed first in aquatic ancestors. Amphibians are not free of their fishy past. Their skin is not equipped for a dry world, and their eggs cannot survive out of water. Today's moist-skinned frogs, toads, and newts still depend on wet habitats for survival.

DEVONIAN SCENE
The Devonian period (416–359 mya), when vertebrates first walked on land, was marked by arid climates in many parts of the world. Lobe-finned fish, the ancestors of tetrapods, were common in shallow lakes and rivers.

WALK ON WATER
Paleontologists have long identified an extinct group of lobe-finned fish, rhipidistians, as ancestors of early tetrapods. Today, some scientists believe the Dipnoi (living and fossil lungfish) are more closely related to tetrapods. For example, if its lake becomes shallow and stagnant, *Neoceratodus* pushes along the lake floor on its fins and breathes air.

Dipterus valenciennesi (a fossil lungfish), Devonian, Scotland

Lungfish *Neoceratodus forsteri* lives only in Australia

FOUR-LEGGED FISH
In many ways, *Tiktaalik* is a fish with legs and other tetrapod-like features. The animal was 10 ft (3 m) long and lived 375 mya. Its skull, neck, ribs, and parts of the limbs were similar to the four-legged tetrapods. But it also had fishlike features, such as a primitive jaw, fins, and scales. Well-preserved fossils have been found in Ellesmere Island in the Nunavut Territory of Canada.

Tiktaalik shows the transition between fish and tetrapod

Strong back

Fin rays on tail

Fish-finned tail

Fishlike scales

Strengthened hip girdle

This model of Ichthyostega *shows five-toed, webbed, paddle feet, but it is now known that each hind foot had seven toes*

Fossil skull of *Acanthostega* Late Devonian Greenland

Spiracle (vent) drew in water

Eye socket

Pocket encloses nostril for drawing in air

Row of tiny teeth

Fishlike tail fin enhanced swimming

Reconstruction of *Acanthostega*

Vertebral column supported strong muscles for swimming

Operculum (gill cover)

Tail

Gill chamber containing gill bars

FISH OUT OF WATER

Discovered in 1952, the fossils of *Acanthostega* show another very early tetrapod. Bearing fishlike gills and a tail with a fin, 3-ft- (1-m-) long *Acanthostega*, like *Tiktaalik*, lived more in water than it did on land. *Acanthostega* and *Tiktaalik* fossils are evidence that feet first developed in aquatic animals, rather than in animals that were already land based. *Acanthostega* probably had lungs, too, filling them with air pumped through its mouth as it crawled onto lake shores or riverbanks.

Toes embedded in rock

Part of pelvis

Femur (thigh bone)

Fibula (calf bone)

Tibia (shin bone)

Clump of three tiny toes

Recently discovered specimen of *Acanthostega*

Eye socket

QUITE A HANDFUL

Five fingers and toes may seem normal, but *Ichthyostega* is now known to have had seven toes on its hind feet rather than the five first suggested. *Acanthostega* had even more toes, with eight on each of its front feet.

Flat, paddle-shaped hind limb of *Ichthyostega* Late Devonian, Greenland

Strong vertebral column supported body weight

Broad pelvic girdle carried muscles that lifted body onto legs

Wide, U-shaped shoulder girdle, separate from back of skull

Skeleton of *Eryops* Permian, Texas, US

BONY BULK

Broad-shouldered, 6-ft- (2-m-) long *Eryops* was an awkward mover on land. Its wide, long, flat skull had sharp, spiky teeth for attacking prey. Two hundred million years after the tetrapods first walked on land, many different kinds of amphibians lived a semiaquatic life. Even for large *Eryops*, however, competition was already present in up-and-coming reptiles.

Model of *Ichthyostega* Late Devonian Greenland

FIN AND FEET

Ichthyostega, another one of the first tetrapods, was 3 ft (1 m) long and lived about 360 mya. Fossils of *Ichthyostega* have been found only in Greenland, where *Acanthostega* was also found. This model shows the generally fishy outline of *Ichthyostega*, even though it was built before the latest fossil finds. A fish-finned tail would have propelled it through the water and, if it walked on land, the same sinuous body movement might have helped it sidle forward to catch prey in its fanglike teeth.

Strong shoulder girdle

Front foot has five toes

Forest swamps

THE SEEDS OF INDUSTRIAL DEVELOPMENT, with its early reliance on coal, were sown about 330 million years ago. In the Carboniferous period, a warm, humid climate prevailed over much of the northern and southern continents and vast swamps supported dense forests of giant, treelike plants. Great thicknesses of dead vegetation were laid down. Over millions of years, they were converted to carbon-rich coal. The Carboniferous coal swamps were filled with 66-ft- (20-m-) tall horsetails, huge ferns, and giant club mosses such as *Lepidodendron*. Each fossilized part of this tree has its own name. The fossils can be combined to rebuild this giant of the forest swamps.

Branch

Thin short leaf

Lepidostrobus cone

Trunk (stem) showing scars left by leaf shed

A *Lepidodendron* reconstruction

Rhizophore

Fine root

Cortex

Pith

Xylem

CROSS-SECTION
The woody part (secondary xylem) of *Lepidodendron's* stem was much thinner than in most of today's trees. The main support (a thick, corklike layer) was the secondary cortex. The center of the stem was filled with spongy pith.

Tip of cone

Cone of *Lepidostrobus* Carboniferous Scotland

UNSTEADY GIANT
Lepidodendron grew rapidly, reaching heights of more than 165 ft (50 m) in a few years. Such tall trees stood above the shade of other plants, their short, grasslike leaves uninterrupted in absorbing the sun's energy. With little supporting wood in their stems, mature *Lepidodendron* trees would have been unsteady and liable to topple, adding to the decaying vegetation on the swamp floor.

Bark pattern of *Lepidodendron* Carboniferous Scotland

Y-shaped branch

Branch of *Lepidodendron* Early Carboniferous England

SPORE CONE
Lepidodendron spread throughout the swamp by releasing tiny spores that were carried over a wide area by wind and then by water. The spores were stored in cones called *Lepidostrobus*. Up to 8 in (20 cm) long, they hung on the ends of branches.

DIAMOND MARKS
Like the tread of a car tire, the diamond-shaped bark pattern of *Lepidodendron* is highly distinctive. The diamonds are cushions at the base of leaves, revealed when the leaves fell off. Arranged in a spiral pattern, the shapes and sizes of the scars vary along the stem to the ends of the branches, showing that the leaves must have been of different sizes, too.

Stigmaria Carboniferous Scotland

Spiral pattern of pits left by rhizophore roots

BRANCHING BRANCHES
Preserved as they were buried by a sudden torrent of sand and water, these branches retain their typical bark pattern. *Lepidodendron* branches divided in two as they grew, producing Y-shaped junctions just as their roots did below. The branches would have been covered in fine leaves during their life.

ROOT AND BRANCH
Just as a fossil bark pattern was named *Lepidodendron* and a fossil cone was named *Lepidostrobus*, so the root-bearing branches, the rhizophores, have their own fossil name, *Stigmaria*. Covered with fine roots arranged in a spiral pattern, these rhizophores absorbed water and supported the *Lepidodendron* trunk in the spongy swamp.

Rhizophore (root-bearing branch)

Two-pronged rhizophore spread outward 40 ft (12 m) or more into swamp

How coal is formed

Coal deposits have built up during many geological periods from the Devonian onward, but those of the Carboniferous are the best known. When swamp plants died and fell into waterlogged soil, the water prevented microorganisms from fully breaking down the plant tissue. Instead it was left as a light, spongy peat, preserving many of the plants and animals found today as fossils. New plants grew on the wet peat surface, piling up more dead plant material when they toppled. Periodic flooding covered this vegetation with layers of sand and mud. Over millions of years, the peat was compressed by rock layers into thick seams of coal.

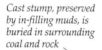

FOSSIL FUEL
Coal has been the power behind the steam-powered engines and the growth of the chemical and transportation industries during the Industrial Revolution of the 1800s. Vast supplies of this high-energy fuel and raw material for products lie underground in many countries—a huge economic resource.

Fossil fuel in the form of a lump of coal

SWAMPS—DEAD OR ALIVE
Carboniferous coal-forming swamps, packed with live and dead vegetation and a variety of animal life, may have looked like the Everglades in Florida. Arthropods fed on rotting vegetation and on each other, while the large predators—the amphibians—were swimming in pools and preying on fish.

Cast stump, preserved by in-filling muds, is buried in surrounding coal and rock

BURIED TREE
Sigillaria was another large tree from the Carboniferous coal swamps. Over 3 ft 3 in (1 m) in diameter, *Sigillaria* had a trunk more than 100 ft (30 m) high and a fringe of long, grasslike leaves hanging from one or two branches. Upright trunk casts found in coal seams show how fast some swamps were flooded with sediments.

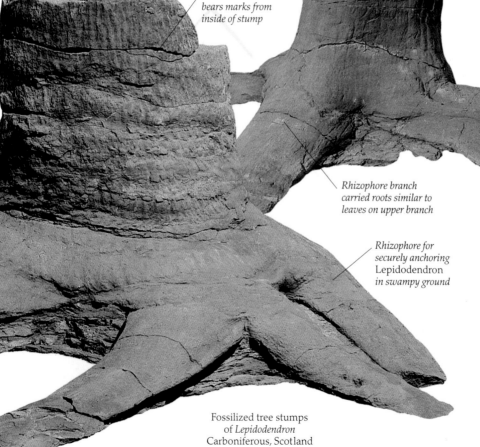

Natural cast bears marks from inside of stump

Rhizophore for drawing water up woody stem

Rhizophore branch carried roots similar to leaves on upper branch

Rhizophore for securely anchoring Lepidodendron *in swampy ground*

FOSSIL GROVE
Lepidodendron trunks and roots still standing where they once grew are not rare. The most famous are a group of 11 in a park in Glasgow, Scotland. These fossils preserve none of the original plant material; they are casts of the inside of the trunk and roots. The trees had broken and their stumps had rotted, leaving only the toughest outer layer. A sand-loaded flood poured enormous quantities of fine sediment into the stand of hollow stumps, filling them down to the roots. The surrounding rock has been removed, leaving the casts standing free.

Fossilized tree stumps of *Lepidodendron*
Carboniferous, Scotland

Reptiles reign

EVEN IF AMPHIBIANS CAN SURVIVE can survive on dry land, they must return to water to lay their soft eggs. Amniotes are animals that freed themselves of this need by producing an egg that enclosed the developing embryo in its own wet world, protecting it with a tough, waterproof shell. Reptiles were the first amniotes, followed by birds and mammals. The first reptiles appeared in the Carboniferous period and may have looked little different from their amphibian ancestors. Unfortunately, internal egg structures were not fossilized. Hence, paleontologists must distinguish between amphibians and early reptiles by skeletal differences.

HOT STUFF
Reptiles adopted many shapes. In the Early Permian period, *Dimetrodon* (a meat-eating pelycosaur) grew to 10 ft (3 m) long and carried a huge fan of skin along its back as a giant radiator and heat absorber.

SETTING SAIL
A plant-eating pelycosaur (sailed lizard), *Edaphosaurus* had a skin-covered sail supported on long vertebral spines with cross pieces, like a ship's mast.

Pelvis, legs, and five-toed feet were separated from trunk

Individual spine in backbone

One of the spines that supported the sail of *Edaphosaurus*, Early Permian, US

Flattened skull

Backbone with ribs attached

REPTILE FIRST
From a small quarry in central Scotland, this distorted 8-in- (20-cm-) long fossil skeleton (nicknamed "Lizzie") is one of the most important fossils ever found. Sandwiched between fine rock layers for 350 million years, *Westlothiana lizziae* is the oldest reptile and amniote known.

Dry, scaly skin

Very long body

Model of *Westlothiana lizziae* (viewed from above), based on scientific research and artist's impression

UNDERSTANDING THE EVIDENCE
Westlothiana was discovered in Early Carboniferous rocks that formed in a lake fed by hot, volcanic spring water. Four-legged, as well as legless, snakelike amphibian skeletons were also found, along with spiders, scorpions, and millipedes. Tree-sized seed ferns grew nearby. *Westlothiana* was about 1 ft (30 cm) long, with short legs. Some, but not all, features of the skull and limb bones match those found in later reptiles. It is not surprising that *Westlothiana*, so similar to its amphibian ancestors, is not easily distinguished from them.

Long, lizardlike tail

Tail made up large part of whole body length

Scales on skin helped keep Westlothiana *waterproof*

Model of *Westlothiana lizziae*, the earliest-known reptile Early Carboniferous Scotland

Each foot had five toes

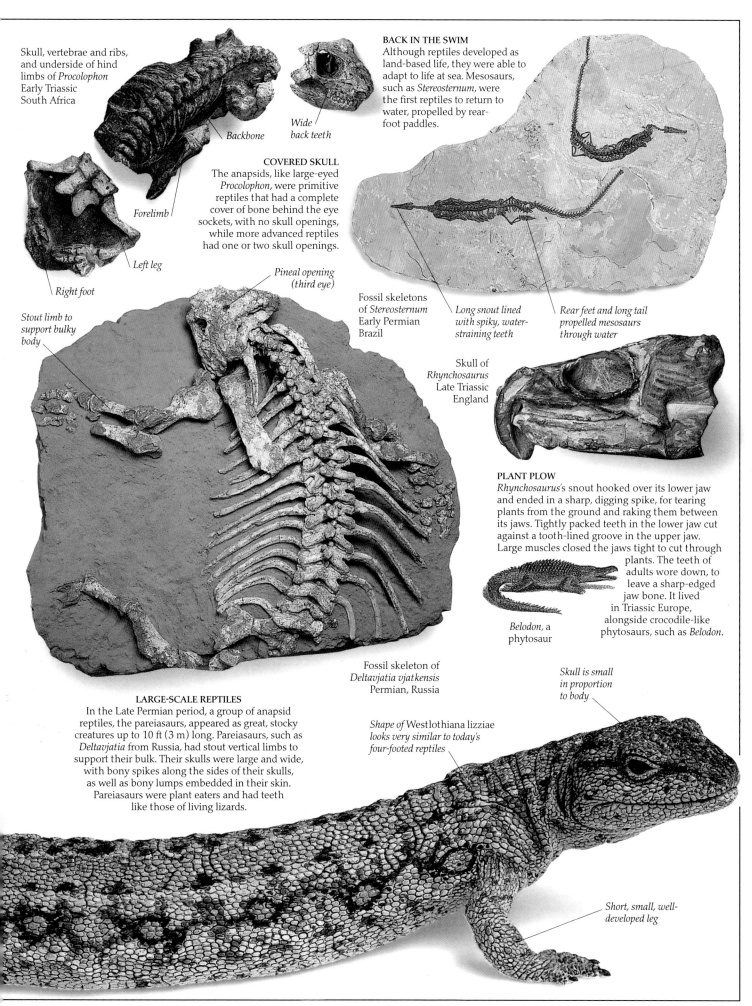

Skull, vertebrae and ribs, and underside of hind limbs of *Procolophon* Early Triassic South Africa

Backbone

Forelimb

Left leg

Right foot

Wide back teeth

COVERED SKULL
The anapsids, like large-eyed *Procolophon*, were primitive reptiles that had a complete cover of bone behind the eye sockets, with no skull openings, while more advanced reptiles had one or two skull openings.

Stout limb to support bulky body

Pineal opening (third eye)

BACK IN THE SWIM
Although reptiles developed as land-based life, they were able to adapt to life at sea. Mesosaurs, such as *Stereosternum*, were the first reptiles to return to water, propelled by rear-foot paddles.

Fossil skeletons of *Stereosternum* Early Permian Brazil

Long snout lined with spiky, water-straining teeth

Rear feet and long tail propelled mesosaurs through water

Skull of *Rhynchosaurus* Late Triassic England

PLANT PLOW
Rhynchosaurus's snout hooked over its lower jaw and ended in a sharp, digging spike, for tearing plants from the ground and raking them between its jaws. Tightly packed teeth in the lower jaw cut against a tooth-lined groove in the upper jaw. Large muscles closed the jaws tight to cut through plants. The teeth of adults wore down, to leave a sharp-edged jaw bone. It lived in Triassic Europe, alongside crocodile-like phytosaurs, such as *Belodon*.

Belodon, a phytosaur

LARGE-SCALE REPTILES
In the Late Permian period, a group of anapsid reptiles, the pareiasaurs, appeared as great, stocky creatures up to 10 ft (3 m) long. Pareiasaurs, such as *Deltavjatia* from Russia, had stout vertical limbs to support their bulk. Their skulls were large and wide, with bony spikes along the sides of their skulls, as well as bony lumps embedded in their skin. Pareiasaurs were plant eaters and had teeth like those of living lizards.

Fossil skeleton of *Deltavjatia vjatkensis* Permian, Russia

Shape of *Westlothiana lizziae* looks very similar to today's four-footed reptiles

Skull is small in proportion to body

Short, small, well-developed leg

Reptiles like mammals

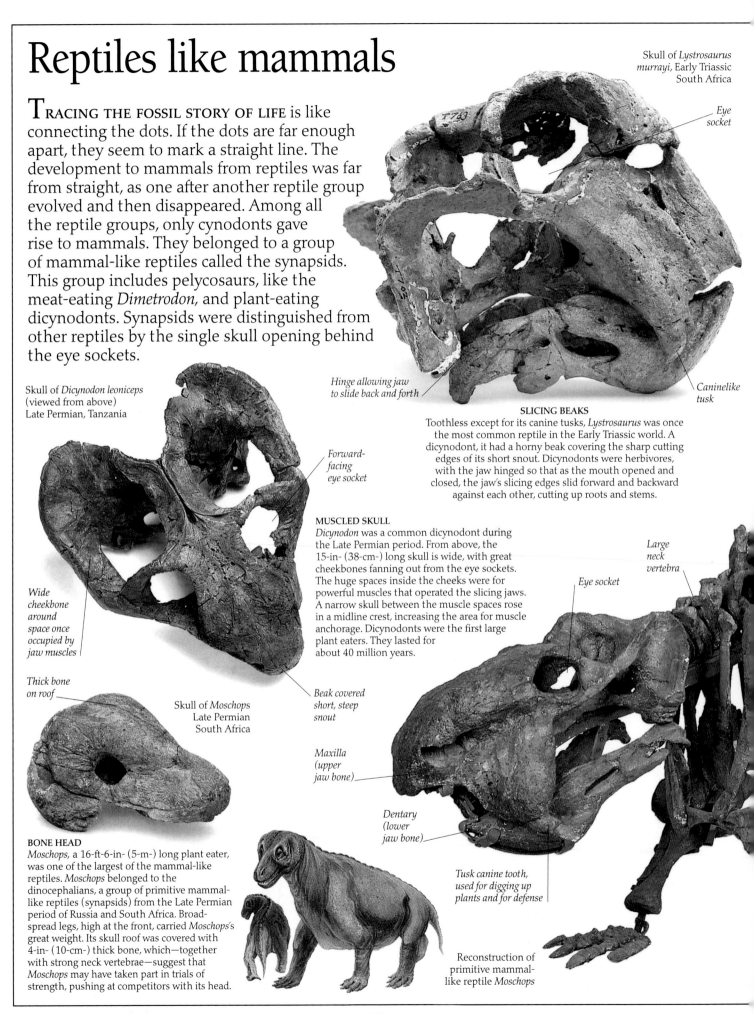

TRACING THE FOSSIL STORY OF LIFE is like connecting the dots. If the dots are far enough apart, they seem to mark a straight line. The development to mammals from reptiles was far from straight, as one after another reptile group evolved and then disappeared. Among all the reptile groups, only cynodonts gave rise to mammals. They belonged to a group of mammal-like reptiles called the synapsids. This group includes pelycosaurs, like the meat-eating *Dimetrodon*, and plant-eating dicynodonts. Synapsids were distinguished from other reptiles by the single skull opening behind the eye sockets.

Skull of *Lystrosaurus murrayi*, Early Triassic South Africa

Eye socket

Hinge allowing jaw to slide back and forth

Caninelike tusk

SLICING BEAKS
Toothless except for its canine tusks, *Lystrosaurus* was once the most common reptile in the Early Triassic world. A dicynodont, it had a horny beak covering the sharp cutting edges of its short snout. Dicynodonts were herbivores, with the jaw hinged so that as the mouth opened and closed, the jaw's slicing edges slid forward and backward against each other, cutting up roots and stems.

Skull of *Dicynodon leoniceps* (viewed from above) Late Permian, Tanzania

Forward-facing eye socket

Wide cheekbone around space once occupied by jaw muscles

MUSCLED SKULL
Dicynodon was a common dicynodont during the Late Permian period. From above, the 15-in- (38-cm-) long skull is wide, with great cheekbones fanning out from the eye sockets. The huge spaces inside the cheeks were for powerful muscles that operated the slicing jaws. A narrow skull between the muscle spaces rose in a midline crest, increasing the area for muscle anchorage. Dicynodonts were the first large plant eaters. They lasted for about 40 million years.

Large neck vertebra

Eye socket

Thick bone on roof

Skull of *Moschops* Late Permian South Africa

Beak covered short, steep snout

Maxilla (upper jaw bone)

Dentary (lower jaw bone)

BONE HEAD
Moschops, a 16-ft-6-in- (5-m-) long plant eater, was one of the largest of the mammal-like reptiles. *Moschops* belonged to the dinocephalians, a group of primitive mammal-like reptiles (synapsids) from the Late Permian period of Russia and South Africa. Broad-spread legs, high at the front, carried *Moschops's* great weight. Its skull roof was covered with 4-in- (10-cm-) thick bone, which—together with strong neck vertebrae—suggest that *Moschops* may have taken part in trials of strength, pushing at competitors with its head.

Tusk canine tooth, used for digging up plants and for defense

Reconstruction of primitive mammal-like reptile *Moschops*

Skull of *Cynognathus crateronotus*
Early Triassic, South Africa
(Karroo Basin)

MAMMAL MOUTH
Up to 16 in (40 cm) in length, the skull of the fierce carnivore *Cynognathus* shows some details that identify cynodonts as the ancestors of mammals. Mammal-like reptiles have different kinds of teeth: small front incisors, large stabbing canines, and broad-back teeth, just as mammals do. Unlike reptiles, mammals have only two sets of teeth.

Large canine tooth

Coarsely serrated cheek tooth

EAR TO EAR
Teeth, jaws, and ears all changed in the development from reptile to mammal. Only mammals can chew, by using special jaw hinges that bring upper and lower teeth together in a precision chewing bite. As the reptile jaw hinge changed in shape and use, some of the small bones were freed to form part of the sensitive mammal ear. The hammer, developed from the articular part of the reptile jaw, vibrates on the anvil. This anvil was once the quadrate (hinge bone) of the reptile skull.

Quadrate

Articular | Skull of reptile, *Dimetrodon*

Quadrate

Articular

Skull of mammal-like reptile, *Thrinaxodon*

MAMMAL-LIKE REPTILE
Cynodonts had aquired many mammal features by the beginning of the Triassic period. Pits in the snout bones of the 18-in- (50-cm-) long carnivore *Thrinaxodon* may have been for sensitive whiskers. It is also possible that *Thrinaxodon* had hair rather than reptile skin. Upright limbs meant a fast, smooth motion.

Reconstruction of *Thrinaxodon*, an Early Triassic cynodont from South Africa

Hammer

Anvil

Eardrum

Mammal ear

Broad shoulder bone for carrying massive trunk

Dorsal vertebra

Neural spine

Ilium (upper hip bone)

DRY BASIN
Many mammal-like fossils come from the Karroo Basin in South Africa. The rocks there are coarse sandstones, often blood-red. Against this dark background, the fossil bones are often preserved as white remains. This part of the world was hot and often dry. Its rocks were deposited between the end of the Permian and the beginning of the Jurassic periods.

Ischium (lower hip bone)

HEAVYWEIGHT HERBIVORES
Sinokannemeyeria was a pig-sized dicynodont from the Early Triassic period of China. Long-snouted, with a low crest behind the eyes for anchoring its jaw muscles, *Sinokannemeyeria* was about 10 ft (3 m) long. The long snout had a sharp, slicing beak and may have housed sensitive smelling organs. Dicynodonts were slow moving. Their sprawling front limbs and large elbows were muscled for lifting their heavy weight rather than for moving at speed. The rear legs turned inward as they pushed forward with long strides.

Thick leg bone supported massive weight of body

Skeleton of *Sinokannemeyeria yinchiaoensis* Triassic, China

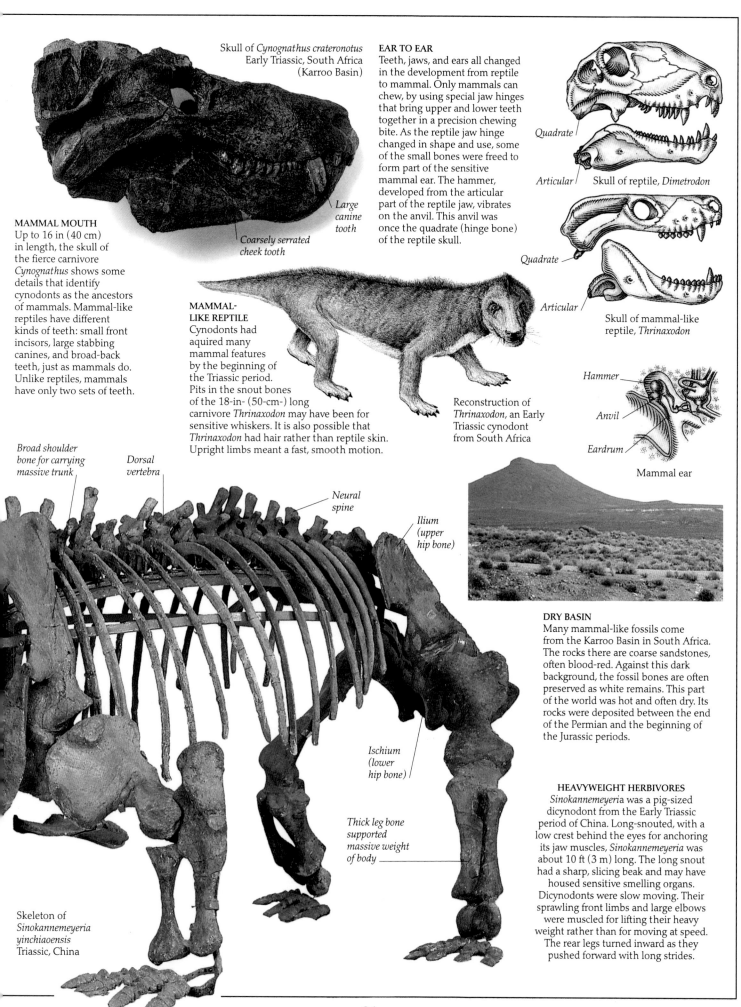

The age of the dinosaurs

GIANT PREDATORS, LUMBERING PLANT PROCESSORS, agile browsers, and pack hunters, dinosaurs occupy a grand place in our knowledge of prehistoric life, featuring in movies, on television, in books, and in toy stores. These amazing reptiles are split into two groups: saurischian (reptile-hipped) and ornithischian (bird-hipped). Their 160-million-year reign left fossilized clues to how they lived, but much remains to be learned about these terrestrial reptiles. Dinosaurs appeared about 230 million years ago and gradually dominated life on land. Their ability to stand upright, grow fast, and breathe efficiently helped them become versatile and adaptable but did not save them from extinction 65 million years ago.

Skull of *Eoraptor* (230 mya), Argentina

FIRST SIGNS
Eoraptor is one of the oldest-known dinosaurs, along with *Eodromaeus* and *Herrerasaurus*. Discovered in Argentina in 1992, this small, 230-million-year-old dinosaur seems to have been a carnivore (meat eater), perhaps the first in a long line of dinosaur terrors.

PROBLEM POSER
Herrerasaurus, also from Argentina, has been described as a theropod dinosaur (a saurischian two-legged carnivore). There is a debate whether it is a true theropod or a primitive saurischian that evolved before theropods split from the rest of the dinosaur family tree.

Model of 10-ft- (3-m-) long *Herrerasaurus* (230 mya) Argentina

DINOSAUR RECORDS
Some dinosaurs—the big sauropods—were the largest animals ever to live on land. *Diplodocus* was one of the longest, at 89 ft (27 m) long. Like other sauropod dinosaurs, it was a huge, four-legged herbivore (plant eater) with a long neck and tail. Sauropods were saurischian dinosaurs, with the two lower bones of the pelvis (the pubis and the ischium) pointing in opposite directions below the pelvic upper bone (the ilium).

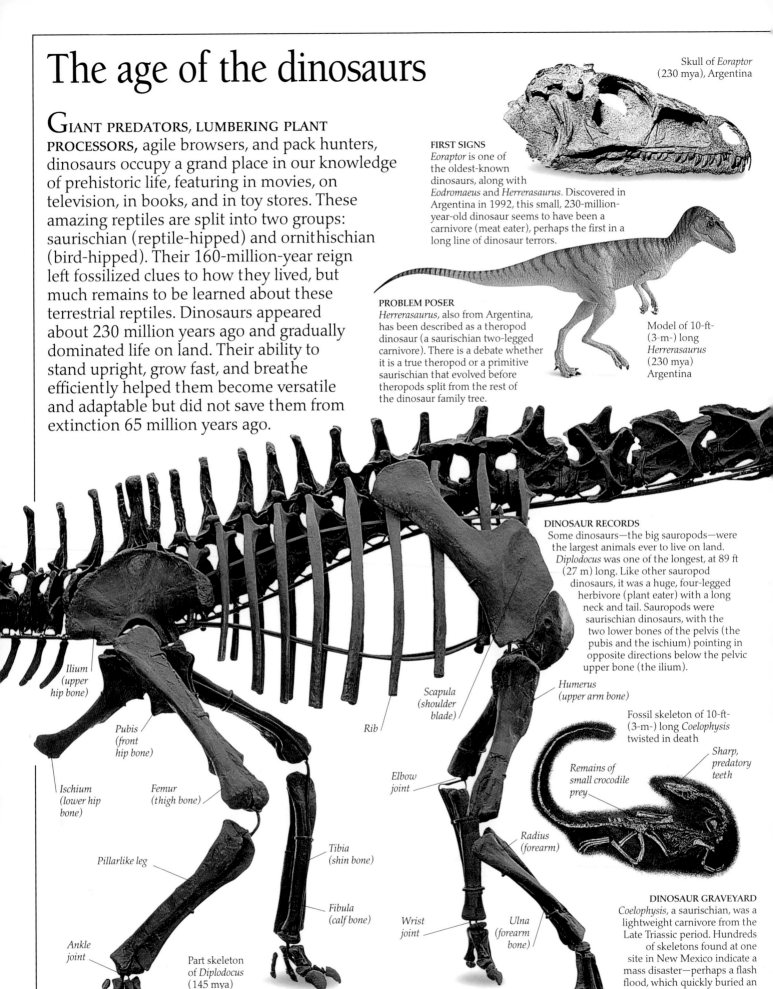

Ilium (upper hip bone)

Pubis (front hip bone)

Ischium (lower hip bone)

Femur (thigh bone)

Pillarlike leg

Tibia (shin bone)

Fibula (calf bone)

Ankle joint

Part skeleton of *Diplodocus* (145 mya) Worldwide

Scapula (shoulder blade)

Rib

Elbow joint

Wrist joint

Ulna (forearm bone)

Radius (forearm)

Humerus (upper arm bone)

Fossil skeleton of 10-ft- (3-m-) long *Coelophysis* twisted in death

Sharp, predatory teeth

Remains of small crocodile prey

DINOSAUR GRAVEYARD
Coelophysis, a saurischian, was a lightweight carnivore from the Late Triassic period. Hundreds of skeletons found at one site in New Mexico indicate a mass disaster—perhaps a flash flood, which quickly buried an entire hunting pack.

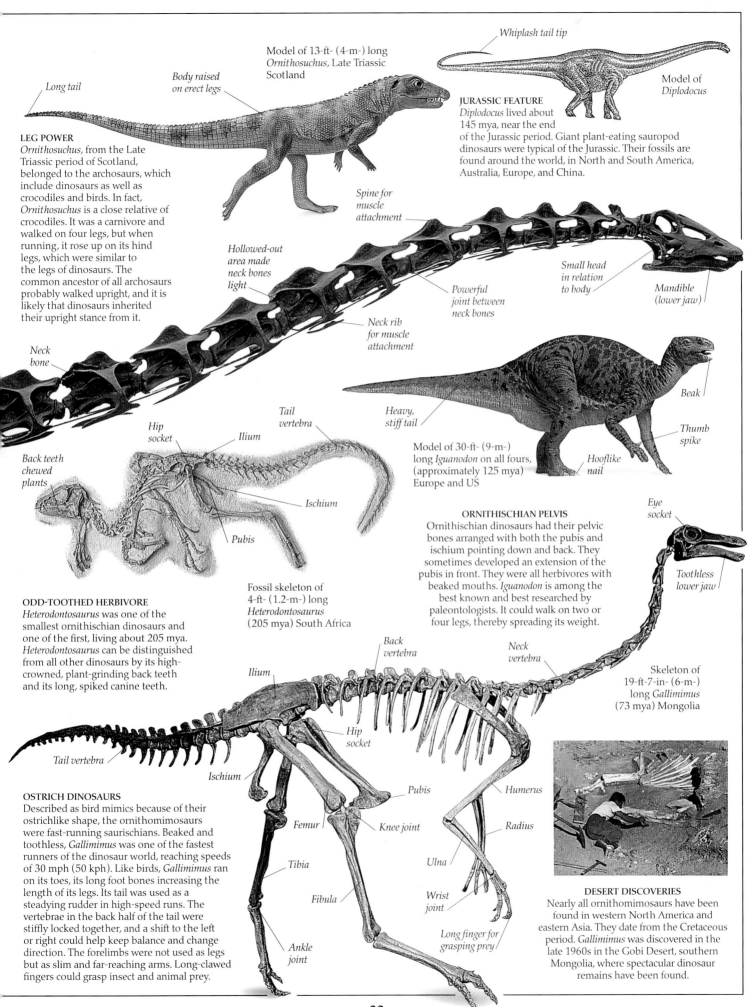

Model of 13-ft- (4-m-) long *Ornithosuchus*, Late Triassic Scotland

Long tail

Body raised on erect legs

LEG POWER
Ornithosuchus, from the Late Triassic period of Scotland, belonged to the archosaurs, which include dinosaurs as well as crocodiles and birds. In fact, *Ornithosuchus* is a close relative of crocodiles. It was a carnivore and walked on four legs, but when running, it rose up on its hind legs, which were similar to the legs of dinosaurs. The common ancestor of all archosaurs probably walked upright, and it is likely that dinosaurs inherited their upright stance from it.

Whiplash tail tip

Model of Diplodocus

JURASSIC FEATURE
Diplodocus lived about 145 mya, near the end of the Jurassic period. Giant plant-eating sauropod dinosaurs were typical of the Jurassic. Their fossils are found around the world, in North and South America, Australia, Europe, and China.

Spine for muscle attachment

Hollowed-out area made neck bones light

Powerful joint between neck bones

Neck rib for muscle attachment

Neck bone

Small head in relation to body

Mandible (lower jaw)

Heavy, stiff tail

Beak

Thumb spike

Model of 30-ft- (9-m-) long *Iguanodon* on all fours, (approximately 125 mya) Europe and US

Hooflike nail

Back teeth chewed plants

Hip socket

Ilium

Tail vertebra

Ischium

Pubis

ODD-TOOTHED HERBIVORE
Heterodontosaurus was one of the smallest ornithischian dinosaurs and one of the first, living about 205 mya. *Heterodontosaurus* can be distinguished from all other dinosaurs by its high-crowned, plant-grinding back teeth and its long, spiked canine teeth.

Fossil skeleton of 4-ft- (1.2-m-) long *Heterodontosaurus* (205 mya) South Africa

ORNITHISCHIAN PELVIS
Ornithischian dinosaurs had their pelvic bones arranged with both the pubis and ischium pointing down and back. They sometimes developed an extension of the pubis in front. They were all herbivores with beaked mouths. *Iguanodon* is among the best known and best researched by paleontologists. It could walk on two or four legs, thereby spreading its weight.

Eye socket

Toothless lower jaw

Back vertebra

Neck vertebra

Ilium

Hip socket

Skeleton of 19-ft-7-in- (6-m-) long *Gallimimus* (73 mya) Mongolia

Tail vertebra

Ischium

Pubis

Humerus

Femur

Knee joint

Radius

OSTRICH DINOSAURS
Described as bird mimics because of their ostrichlike shape, the ornithomimosaurs were fast-running saurischians. Beaked and toothless, *Gallimimus* was one of the fastest runners of the dinosaur world, reaching speeds of 30 mph (50 kph). Like birds, *Gallimimus* ran on its toes, its long foot bones increasing the length of its legs. Its tail was used as a steadying rudder in high-speed runs. The vertebrae in the back half of the tail were stiffly locked together, and a shift to the left or right could help keep balance and change direction. The forelimbs were not used as legs but as slim and far-reaching arms. Long-clawed fingers could grasp insect and animal prey.

Tibia

Ulna

Fibula

Wrist joint

Long finger for grasping prey

Ankle joint

DESERT DISCOVERIES
Nearly all ornithomimosaurs have been found in western North America and eastern Asia. They date from the Cretaceous period. *Gallimimus* was discovered in the late 1960s in the Gobi Desert, southern Mongolia, where spectacular dinosaur remains have been found.

33

Saurischians

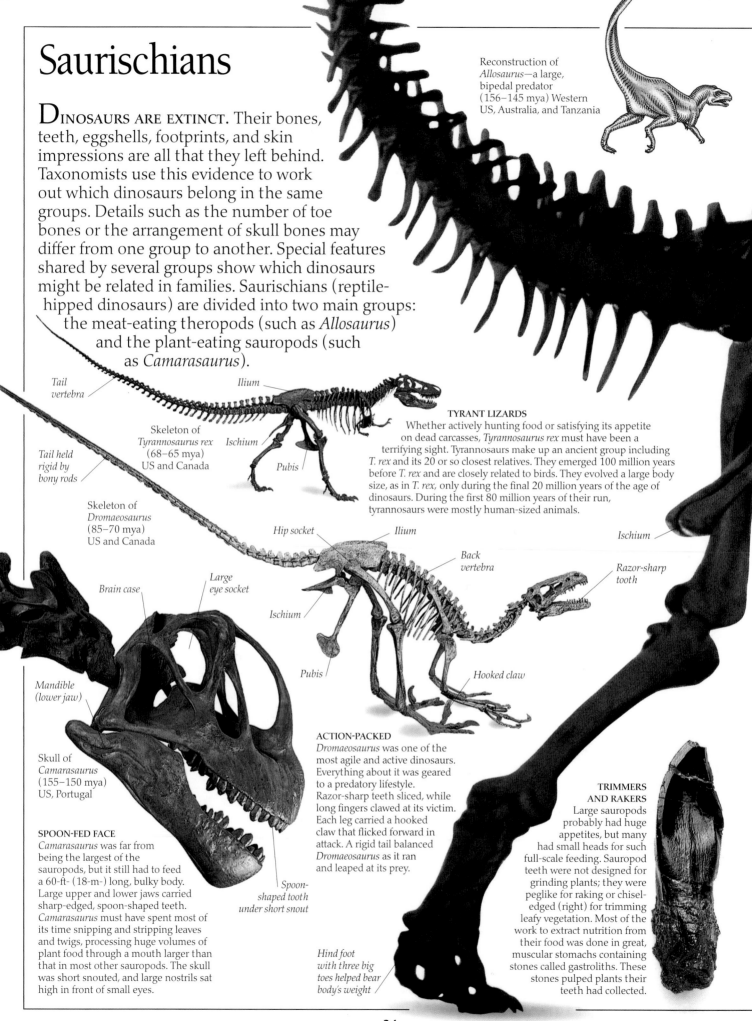

DINOSAURS ARE EXTINCT. Their bones, teeth, eggshells, footprints, and skin impressions are all that they left behind. Taxonomists use this evidence to work out which dinosaurs belong in the same groups. Details such as the number of toe bones or the arrangement of skull bones may differ from one group to another. Special features shared by several groups show which dinosaurs might be related in families. Saurischians (reptile-hipped dinosaurs) are divided into two main groups: the meat-eating theropods (such as *Allosaurus*) and the plant-eating sauropods (such as *Camarasaurus*).

Reconstruction of *Allosaurus*—a large, bipedal predator (156–145 mya) Western US, Australia, and Tanzania

Tail vertebra

Ilium

Skeleton of *Tyrannosaurus rex* (68–65 mya) US and Canada

Ischium

Pubis

Tail held rigid by bony rods

Skeleton of *Dromaeosaurus* (85–70 mya) US and Canada

Hip socket

Ilium

Back vertebra

Ischium

Razor-sharp tooth

Ischium

Pubis

Hooked claw

Brain case

Large eye socket

Mandible (lower jaw)

Skull of *Camarasaurus* (155–150 mya) US, Portugal

TYRANT LIZARDS

Whether actively hunting food or satisfying its appetite on dead carcasses, *Tyrannosaurus rex* must have been a terrifying sight. Tyrannosaurs make up an ancient group including *T. rex* and its 20 or so closest relatives. They emerged 100 million years before *T. rex* and are closely related to birds. They evolved a large body size, as in *T. rex*, only during the final 20 million years of the age of dinosaurs. During the first 80 million years of their run, tyrannosaurs were mostly human-sized animals.

ACTION-PACKED

Dromaeosaurus was one of the most agile and active dinosaurs. Everything about it was geared to a predatory lifestyle. Razor-sharp teeth sliced, while long fingers clawed at its victim. Each leg carried a hooked claw that flicked forward in attack. A rigid tail balanced *Dromaeosaurus* as it ran and leaped at its prey.

SPOON-FED FACE

Camarasaurus was far from being the largest of the sauropods, but it still had to feed a 60-ft- (18-m-) long, bulky body. Large upper and lower jaws carried sharp-edged, spoon-shaped teeth. *Camarasaurus* must have spent most of its time snipping and stripping leaves and twigs, processing huge volumes of plant food through a mouth larger than that in most other sauropods. The skull was short snouted, and large nostrils sat high in front of small eyes.

Spoon-shaped tooth under short snout

Hind foot with three big toes helped bear body's weight

TRIMMERS AND RAKERS

Large sauropods probably had huge appetites, but many had small heads for such full-scale feeding. Sauropod teeth were not designed for grinding plants; they were peglike for raking or chisel-edged (right) for trimming leafy vegetation. Most of the work to extract nutrition from their food was done in great, muscular stomachs containing stones called gastroliths. These stones pulped plants their teeth had collected.

SAUROPOD PREVIEW
Before the sauropods appeared, an earlier group of small saurischian dinosaurs made their mark in the Late Triassic period, about 230 mya. These prosauropods were never much longer than 33 ft (10 m). Many had small heads on long necks. *Plateosaurus* was able to rise on its hind legs, but it normally stood on all fours—on five-toed feet and five-fingered hands. Its serrated (sawlike) teeth are like the plant-cutting teeth of some modern lizards.

Ilium

Pubis

Ischium

Skeleton of *Plateosaurus*, a 20–26-ft- (6–8-m-) long, four-footed plant eater (220 mya) Germany, France, and Switzerland

Huge, gaping jaw

Bladelike teeth

Curved, long thumb claw may have hooked leaves into mouth

Ilium

Pubis

Large hind limb bore weight of huge body

JURASSIC PREDATOR
Late Cretaceous *Tyrannosaurus* is famous, but 85 million years earlier during the Late Jurassic period, *Allosaurus* was the big-game hunter. Weighing 1.7–2.2 tons (1.5–2 metric tons) and up to 50 ft (15 m) long, *Allosaurus* took its prey from the groups of sauropods, such as *Barosaurus*, that lived on the North American flood plains. After a short but furious chase, knife-edged teeth and clawed hands delivered the deadly strokes.

Long, low-sloping head

BROWSING *BAROSAURUS*
Not all paleontologists believe that the sauropod *Barosaurus* could have risen up on its hind legs in defense against an attacker, but if it did, it would have towered 50 ft (15 m) above the ground. *Barosaurus* lived alongside the slightly longer *Diplodocus* (pp. 32–33) about 150 mya in Utah and South Dakota. It has also been found in Tanzania.

Running skeleton of *Allosaurus*

Three-fingered hand with huge claw

Powerful forelimbs

FEATHERED THEROPOD
Today, paleontologists believe that most, if not all, theropods were feathered dinosaurs. Several fossils of *Citipati* were discovered in the Gobi Desert in southern Mongolia. It had a short beak and no real teeth. *Citipati* belongs to a group called the oviraptorids, named after a similar creature named *Oviraptor*, or "egg thief." It was partly carnivorous and incubated its eggs, protecting them with its feathered forelimbs.

Body covered with short filaments, probably fur

Rearing up on hind legs in defense or to eat leaves from tall trees

Forearms fringed with long feathers

Whiplash tail for defense

Hallux (a small, first toe turned back behind foot)

Model of *Citipati* (83–70 mya) Mongolia

Ornithischians

ORNITHISCHIAN (BIRD-HIPPED) DINOSAURS had many features in common. Large or small, they were all herbivores, feeding on leaves, fruit, seeds, even conifer needles. Teeth were arranged for slicing and grinding, but ornithischians were toothless at the front of their mouths. A sharp-edged beak did the cutting and tearing instead. All ornithischians had an extra bone, the predentary, at the front of the lower jaw. Another bone unique to ornithischians was the palpebral, in the eyelid. Many ornithischians, like the hadrosaurs, were somewhat bipedal—they walked on their hind legs.

Thick-domed skull rammed against competitor in trial of strength

Bony shelf

Model of 8-ft- (2.4-m-) long *Stegoceras* from fossils found in Montana, US, and in Alberta, Canada (87–67 mya)

Scaly skin

Heavy, stiffened tail for balance

BONEHEAD
Thick-headed and lightly built, *Stegoceras* was first recognized in 1902. It belonged to the pachycephalosaurs, also known as the boneheads, a group of plant-eating dinosaurs with a distinctive, thick-domed skull. The earliest pachycephalosaur comes from the Early Cretaceous period, but most lived during the Late Cretaceous. All were found in North America. Pachycephalosaurs were bipedal, walking only on hind legs.

Long, backswept bony crest of hollow tubes, which produced sounds like a trombone

Ilium

Fossil skeleton of 33-ft- (10-m-) long *Parasaurolophus* (75 mya), North America

Ischium

HORN PLAYER
Parasaurolophus was a large-crested hadrosaur. Hadrosaurs, also known as the duck-billed dinosaurs, were large ornithischians that lived about 75 mya, in the Late Cretaceous period. They had broad, flattened mouths packed with hundreds of teeth. The jaws moved not only up and down but also from side to side. This helped teeth slide over each other and grind tough plant parts to pulp.

Front part of pubis

Body blood was heated or cooled through plates

Part skeleton of 23-ft- (7-m-) long *Tuojiangosaurus* (156 mya) China

Ilium

Dorsal (back) plates—in two rows arranged side by side

Tail vertebra

Ischium

Pubis

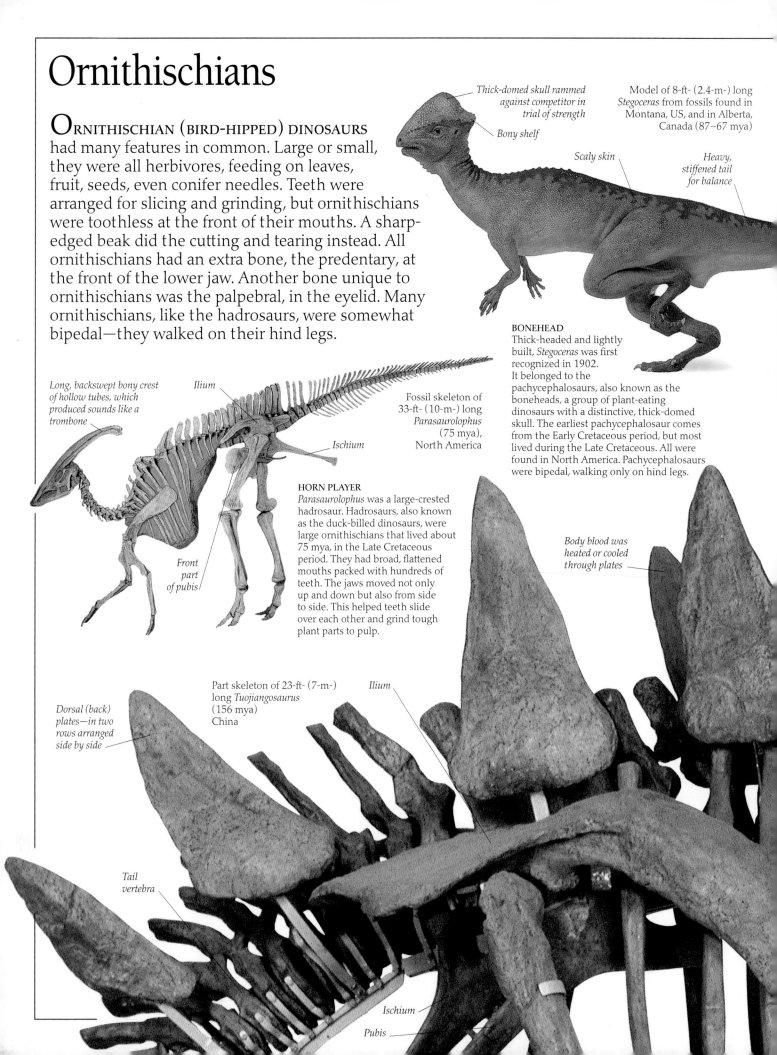

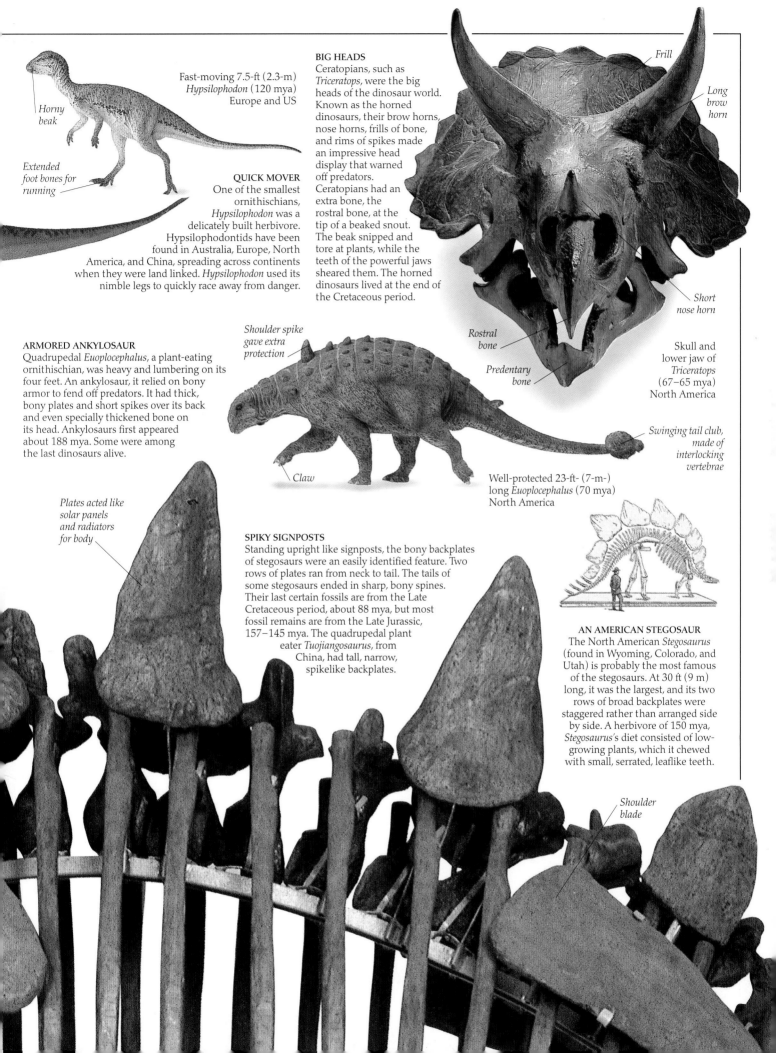

Fast-moving 7.5-ft (2.3-m)
Hypsilophodon (120 mya)
Europe and US

Horny beak

Extended foot bones for running

QUICK MOVER
One of the smallest ornithischians, *Hypsilophodon* was a delicately built herbivore. Hypsilophodontids have been found in Australia, Europe, North America, and China, spreading across continents when they were land linked. *Hypsilophodon* used its nimble legs to quickly race away from danger.

BIG HEADS
Ceratopians, such as *Triceratops*, were the big heads of the dinosaur world. Known as the horned dinosaurs, their brow horns, nose horns, frills of bone, and rims of spikes made an impressive head display that warned off predators. Ceratopians had an extra bone, the rostral bone, at the tip of a beaked snout. The beak snipped and tore at plants, while the teeth of the powerful jaws sheared them. The horned dinosaurs lived at the end of the Cretaceous period.

Frill

Long brow horn

Short nose horn

Rostral bone

Predentary bone

Skull and lower jaw of *Triceratops* (67–65 mya) North America

ARMORED ANKYLOSAUR
Quadrupedal *Euoplocephalus*, a plant-eating ornithischian, was heavy and lumbering on its four feet. An ankylosaur, it relied on bony armor to fend off predators. It had thick, bony plates and short spikes over its back and even specially thickened bone on its head. Ankylosaurs first appeared about 188 mya. Some were among the last dinosaurs alive.

Shoulder spike gave extra protection

Claw

Swinging tail club, made of interlocking vertebrae

Well-protected 23-ft- (7-m-) long *Euoplocephalus* (70 mya) North America

Plates acted like solar panels and radiators for body

SPIKY SIGNPOSTS
Standing upright like signposts, the bony backplates of stegosaurs were an easily identified feature. Two rows of plates ran from neck to tail. The tails of some stegosaurs ended in sharp, bony spines. Their last certain fossils are from the Late Cretaceous period, about 88 mya, but most fossil remains are from the Late Jurassic, 157–145 mya. The quadrupedal plant eater *Tuojiangosaurus*, from China, had tall, narrow, spikelike backplates.

AN AMERICAN STEGOSAUR
The North American *Stegosaurus* (found in Wyoming, Colorado, and Utah) is probably the most famous of the stegosaurs. At 30 ft (9 m) long, it was the largest, and its two rows of broad backplates were staggered rather than arranged side by side. A herbivore of 150 mya, *Stegosaurus*'s diet consisted of low-growing plants, which it chewed with small, serrated, leaflike teeth.

Shoulder blade

Reptiles at sea

COMMERCIAL COLLECTOR
Mary Anning (1799–1847) was one of the first commercial fossil collectors. She lived on England's south coast in the seaside town of Lyme Regis, where the rocks are Jurassic in age, and collected fossils to be sold in her father's curiosity shop. She is credited with finding her first ichthyosaur specimen at the age of 11. Many museums have specimens of marine reptiles that Mary Anning discovered.

AFTER LIVING ON LAND for over 80 million years, various reptiles independently adopted a fully aquatic life and dominated the Mesozoic seas as swimming predators. As air-breathing reptiles, they had to surface to fill their lungs, but many features of sight, smell, and respiration became adapted to a marine environment. In marine reptiles, the bones of walking limbs and feet developed into a variety of paddle shapes used as underwater oars or wings. Some reptiles, like turtles, still hauled themselves onto land to lay eggs; underwater, the embryos would suffocate from lack of oxygen. One group of marine reptiles, the ichthyosaurs, cut themselves off from land completely and gave birth to live young (pp. 52–53) in the water.

Most flexible vertebrae in neck

Skeleton of
Cryptoclidus eurymerus
Middle Jurassic
England

Flat, rigid pelvic girdle

Belly ribs strengthened underside of body

Flat-ended femur joined with pelvis

Huge flipper made up of five elongated toes

MARINE FLIER
Plesiosaurs came in two sizes: short-necked, large-headed pliosaurs and long-necked, small-headed plesiosaurids. The jaws of long-necked *Cryptoclidus* had long, spiked teeth that interlocked like two combs when they closed around a fish. The shoulder and pelvic bones were massive, forming a rigid anchorage for the tapered flippers. Some scientists believe that the flippers paddled back and forth, while others think they were used for underwater flight, as with penguins and some turtles.

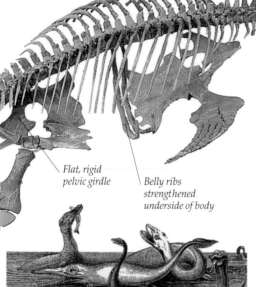

ACTION-PACKED
Although this scene is rather fanciful, the Mesozoic era was a time when reptiles ruled the sea, land, and air. The largest marine reptiles preyed on other reptiles, while smaller swimmers fed on fish or specialized in squid or mollusks. Turtles and crocodiles survived the extinction that befell most marine reptiles.

Stenopterygius quadricissus
Early Jurassic, Germany

Back paddle of
Protostega gigas,
an ancient turtle

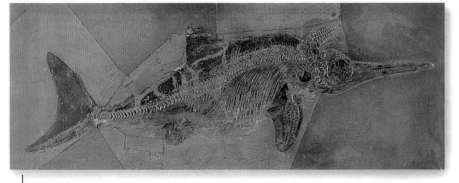

STREAMLINED SWIMMER
This skin impression of *Stenopterygius* displays the features of the highly effective ichthyosaurs, so perfectly shaped for life at sea. Streamlined for speed, *ichthyosaurs* were propelled by the sideways motion of a vertical, sharklike tail. Their flippers were used to stabilize and steer. A long, tooth-lined snout suggests comparisons with modern dolphins, not just in their diet of squid and fish, but also in their active leaping above the waves. A large ring of bones surrounded *Stenopterygius's* huge eyes, suggesting that it had sharp vision in the deep, dark waters.

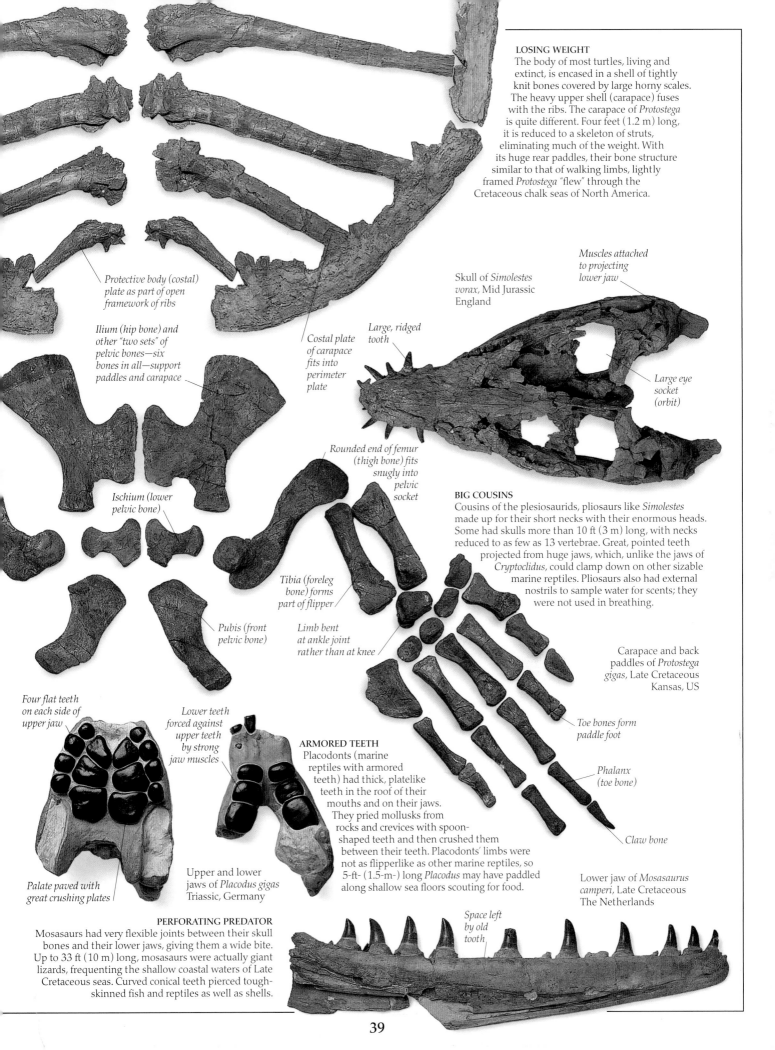

LOSING WEIGHT

The body of most turtles, living and extinct, is encased in a shell of tightly knit bones covered by large horny scales. The heavy upper shell (carapace) fuses with the ribs. The carapace of *Protostega* is quite different. Four feet (1.2 m) long, it is reduced to a skeleton of struts, eliminating much of the weight. With its huge rear paddles, their bone structure similar to that of walking limbs, lightly framed *Protostega* "flew" through the Cretaceous chalk seas of North America.

Protective body (costal) plate as part of open framework of ribs

Ilium (hip bone) and other "two sets" of pelvic bones—six bones in all—support paddles and carapace

Costal plate of carapace fits into perimeter plate

Large, ridged tooth

Muscles attached to projecting lower jaw

Skull of Simolestes vorax, Mid Jurassic England

Large eye socket (orbit)

Ischium (lower pelvic bone)

Rounded end of femur (thigh bone) fits snugly into pelvic socket

BIG COUSINS

Cousins of the plesiosaurids, pliosaurs like *Simolestes* made up for their short necks with their enormous heads. Some had skulls more than 10 ft (3 m) long, with necks reduced to as few as 13 vertebrae. Great, pointed teeth projected from huge jaws, which, unlike the jaws of *Cryptoclidus*, could clamp down on other sizable marine reptiles. Pliosaurs also had external nostrils to sample water for scents; they were not used in breathing.

Tibia (foreleg bone) forms part of flipper

Pubis (front pelvic bone)

Limb bent at ankle joint rather than at knee

Carapace and back paddles of Protostega gigas, Late Cretaceous Kansas, US

Toe bones form paddle foot

Four flat teeth on each side of upper jaw

Lower teeth forced against upper teeth by strong jaw muscles

Phalanx (toe bone)

ARMORED TEETH

Placodonts (marine reptiles with armored teeth) had thick, platelike teeth in the roof of their mouths and on their jaws. They pried mollusks from rocks and crevices with spoon-shaped teeth and then crushed them between their teeth. Placodonts' limbs were not as flipperlike as other marine reptiles, so 5-ft- (1.5-m-) long *Placodus* may have paddled along shallow sea floors scouting for food.

Claw bone

Palate paved with great crushing plates

Upper and lower jaws of Placodus gigas Triassic, Germany

Lower jaw of Mosasaurus camperi, Late Cretaceous The Netherlands

PERFORATING PREDATOR

Mosasaurs had very flexible joints between their skull bones and their lower jaws, giving them a wide bite. Up to 33 ft (10 m) long, mosasaurs were actually giant lizards, frequenting the shallow coastal waters of Late Cretaceous seas. Curved conical teeth pierced tough-skinned fish and reptiles as well as shells.

Space left by old tooth

Flying reptiles

THE LARGEST FLIERS EVER were pterosaurs, which took to the skies in the Triassic period. These archosaur reptiles, closely related to dinosaurs, had wings of reinforced skin stretched across one long finger and powerful muscles. Although pterosaurs had lightweight frames of hollow, air-filled bone, some weighed up to 220 lb (100 kg). There are two main kinds of pterosaurs. The earlier were long-tailed, short-headed rhamphorhynchoids (like *Rhamphorhynchus*). These died out at the end of the Jurassic period, but not before the pterodactyloids had appeared. These short-tailed, long-headed pterosaurs survived until extinction at the end of the Cretaceous period.

SEA FOOD
Fossilized food has been found in the stomachs of several pterosaur remains. Most pterosaur fossils (such as Early Cretaceous *Anhanguera* from Brazil) are found in rocks deposited in shallow seas and some contain fish fossils. *Anhanguera's* long jaws were ideal for scooping up a slippery catch as it flew low over the water. Crests on its beak helped stabilize its head as it dipped into the sea.

FLIGHT ENGINEER
How *Quetzalcoatlus*, with a wingspan of 40 ft (12 m) and weighing as much as 190 lb (86 kg), could carry itself through the air is a miracle of natural engineering. Named after a feathered Aztec god, the long-necked and toothless *Quetzalcoatlus* is the largest pterosaur known. It was far larger than today's giant albatross.

Typical long neck of a pterodactyloid

Model of *Quetzalcoatlus* (65 mya). Its fossil remains were first found in 1971 in Texas.

An enormous 40-ft (12-m) wingspan supported Quetzalcoatlus *in the air*

Wings of Ornithocheirus would have been folded back when not flying

Hollow finger bone reduced weight of wing

Small fragments of bones are pieced together to build complete finger

Only the first joint of the wing finger could bend; the rest of the finger remained rigid

Fourth finger

Wing bone of *Rhamphorhynchus* (160–144 mya) Germany

WING FIBERS
As if stretched out to show its papery fragility, the wrinkled wing of *Rhamphorhynchus* reveals its secret strength. The long fourth finger leads the wing edge. Fine, tough fibers reinforce the membrane of skin. These fibers help stretch and strengthen the skin to withstand the strain as the wing flapped.

Flight muscles attached to a large crest on the humerus

Wing membrane

Terminal vane (rudder) on tail

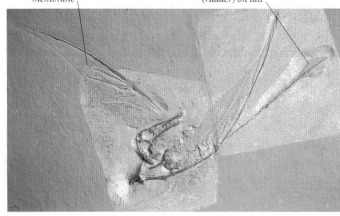

FALLEN FLIER
Famous for its many superb fossils, the Solnhofen Limestone (pp. 42–43) seems to have captured this *Rhamphorhynchus* as it fell to its death (left). A common pterosaur from the Jurassic period, with a wingspan of up to 5 ft 9 in (1.75 m), *Rhamphorhynchus* stabilized and perhaps steered itself with its long-tailed rudder. Flight muscles were attached to a large-keeled breastbone (sternum), as in flying birds. Ribs joined the breastbone to make a strong frame. The shoulder bones (shoulder blade and coracoid) braced the powerful wing movements against the body frame.

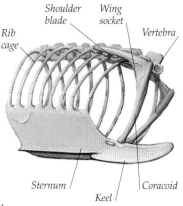

Shoulder blade *Wing socket* *Vertebra*
Rib cage

Sternum *Keel* *Coracoid*

Breastbone of *Rhamphorhynchus*

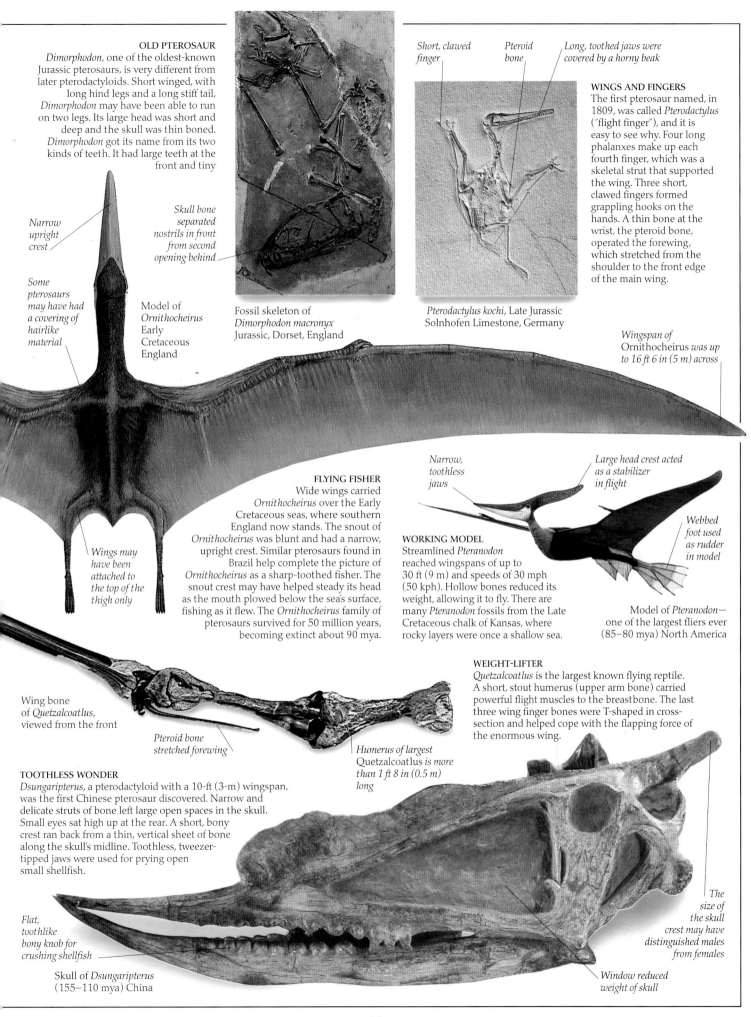

OLD PTEROSAUR

Dimorphodon, one of the oldest-known Jurassic pterosaurs, is very different from later pterodactyloids. Short winged, with long hind legs and a long stiff tail, *Dimorphodon* may have been able to run on two legs. Its large head was short and deep and the skull was thin boned. *Dimorphodon* got its name from its two kinds of teeth. It had large teeth at the front and tiny

Narrow upright crest

Some pterosaurs may have had a covering of hairlike material

Model of *Ornithocheirus* Early Cretaceous England

Skull bone separated nostrils in front from second opening behind

Fossil skeleton of *Dimorphodon macronyx* Jurassic, Dorset, England

Short, clawed finger

Pteroid bone

Long, toothed jaws were covered by a horny beak

WINGS AND FINGERS

The first pterosaur named, in 1809, was called *Pterodactylus* ("flight finger"), and it is easy to see why. Four long phalanxes make up each fourth finger, which was a skeletal strut that supported the wing. Three short, clawed fingers formed grappling hooks on the hands. A thin bone at the wrist, the pteroid bone, operated the forewing, which stretched from the shoulder to the front edge of the main wing.

Pterodactylus kochi, Late Jurassic Solnhofen Limestone, Germany

Wingspan of Ornithocheirus *was up to 16 ft 6 in (5 m) across*

FLYING FISHER

Wide wings carried *Ornithocheirus* over the Early Cretaceous seas, where southern England now stands. The snout of *Ornithocheirus* was blunt and had a narrow, upright crest. Similar pterosaurs found in Brazil help complete the picture of *Ornithocheirus* as a sharp-toothed fisher. The snout crest may have helped steady its head as the mouth plowed below the sea's surface, fishing as it flew. The *Ornithocheirus* family of pterosaurs survived for 50 million years, becoming extinct about 90 mya.

Wings may have been attached to the top of the thigh only

Narrow, toothless jaws

Large head crest acted as a stabilizer in flight

Webbed foot used as rudder in model

WORKING MODEL

Streamlined *Pteranodon* reached wingspans of up to 30 ft (9 m) and speeds of 30 mph (50 kph). Hollow bones reduced its weight, allowing it to fly. There are many *Pteranodon* fossils from the Late Cretaceous chalk of Kansas, where rocky layers were once a shallow sea.

Model of *Pteranodon*— one of the largest fliers ever (85–80 mya) North America

Wing bone of *Quetzalcoatlus*, viewed from the front

Pteroid bone stretched forewing

Humerus of largest Quetzalcoatlus *is more than 1 ft 8 in (0.5 m) long*

WEIGHT-LIFTER

Quetzalcoatlus is the largest known flying reptile. A short, stout humerus (upper arm bone) carried powerful flight muscles to the breastbone. The last three wing finger bones were T-shaped in cross-section and helped cope with the flapping force of the enormous wing.

TOOTHLESS WONDER

Dsungaripterus, a pterodactyloid with a 10-ft (3-m) wingspan, was the first Chinese pterosaur discovered. Narrow and delicate struts of bone left large open spaces in the skull. Small eyes sat high up at the rear. A short, bony crest ran back from a thin, vertical sheet of bone along the skull's midline. Toothless, tweezer-tipped jaws were used for prying open small shellfish.

Flat, toothlike bony knob for crushing shellfish

Skull of *Dsungaripterus* (155–110 mya) China

The size of the skull crest may have distinguished males from females

Window reduced weight of skull

Early birds

BIRDS POSSESS ONE FEATURE found in no other living animal: feathers. The first fossil evidence of birds was a 147-million-year-old feather. The earliest bird, *Archaeopteryx* ("ancient wing"), has perfectly formed feathers preserved as fossils. Feathers started out as simple filaments in feathered dinosaurs, gradually becoming more and more complex. Feathers were useful for body insulation before they became useful for flight. Birds are now recognized as the closest living relatives of dinosaurs. Scientists have found over 100 features common to both *Archaeopteryx* and small theropod dinosaurs (pp. 32–35). Eleven specimens of *Archaeopteryx* have been found since 1861; they are among the world's most famous and precious fossils.

Crow's skeleton

Wishbone made of two joined collar bones

Upper wing bone

Keel anchors wing muscles

FLYING FOOD
Birds are not the only animals that fly. The Late Jurassic skies would have had a wide range of insect life, such as this dragonfly (*Libellula* from Solnhofen in Germany), hunting for food in water or on land. Some scientists think *Archaeopteryx* may have used its feathers as fly swatters!

Lightly built skull with sharp, spiked teeth

Long, flexible neck folded back in death

Three-fingered, clawed hand on delicate arm

Slender, long-toed running leg

FEATHERED DINOSAUR
One particular specimen of *Archaeopteryx* that had left few, if any, feather impressions was identified for many years as this dinosaur, *Compsognathus* (found in the same rock deposits). That some dinosaurs and birds are so hard to tell apart reinforces the idea that birds and dinosaurs are closely related.

AIRCRAFT FRAME
Today's flying birds have a large-keeled breastbone that anchors strong wing muscles and a wishbone that buttresses the wing joints.

Slim finger with sharp claw on end

Birdlike arm carried flight feathers

Large eye socket and brain in lightweight skull

RARE FOSSILS
Eight specimens of *Archaeopteryx* have been found in quarries of Solnhofen Limestone in Germany. The rocks contain fossils of insects, pterosaurs, and dinosaurs.

BERLIN *ARCHAEOPTERYX*
Discovered in 1877, this specimen of *Archaeopteryx* (now in Berlin's Humboldt Museum in Germany) is the most complete. Perfect feather impressions identify it as a bird. The birdlike foot has four sharply clawed toes. Its long, narrow skull has sharp, reptilian teeth but no beak. Feathers fringe a long tailbone, unlike the short, stumpy one of today's birds. The winged arms end in three clawed fingers.

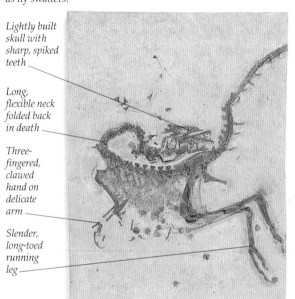

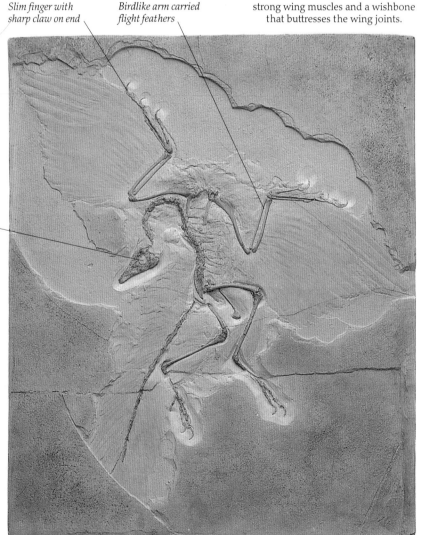

LONDON *ARCHAEOPTERYX*
The first skeleton of *Archaeopteryx* to be found was the London specimen, bought by Britain's Natural History Museum for £700 ($1,100), together with other Solnhofen fossils. Although not so complete as the Berlin *Archaeopteryx*, the London specimen has a well-fossilized wishbone, or furcula (joined collar bones). The discovery of collar bones in some dinosaurs helped convince scientists that birds are the closest living relatives of extinct dinosaurs.

Thin, V-shaped wishbone of fused collar bones

BIRD WATCHER
In 1861, Hermann von Meyer, of Frankfurt, Germany, described the first fossil evidence for birds, a feather, and announced the discovery of the first-known feathered bird, *Archaeopteryx*.

Archaeopteryx spreading its wings

Long leg bone carefully exposed in limestone

Widespread fan of tail feather impressions

FIRST IMPRESSION
In 1860, a beautifully detailed feather imprint, exactly like a modern bird's flight feather, was discovered in a German quarry. A year later, paleontologist Hermann von Meyer published a scientific description of it.

UP OR DOWN
Archaeopteryx provokes one particular question about flight: did birds first spring into the air from a running start, or did they launch themselves from the branches of trees? Some scientists have argued that long, running legs were an advantage for ground takeoff, but others believe that gliding down from tree perches triggered the development of bird flight.

Archaeopteryx fossil feather

Narrow leading edge

Narrow feather tip slows bird when spread in flight

FLIGHT CONTROL
Feathers may have developed from scales as a way of insulating an animal's vital body heat. Eventually, as a group of small, meat-eating dinosaurs (pp. 32–33) evolved into birds, feathers that function as important aerodynamic features were developed.

Wider trailing edge

Crow's wing feather

Skull up to 19 in (48 cm) long

Beak ended in a fierce hook

FLIGHTLESS KILLER
One of the most ferocious birds ever was giant *Phorusrhacus*, a flightless hunter of the South American plains with strong legs and a sharp, hooked beak. In the Early Cenozoic, *Phorusrhacus* and its relatives—some almost as tall as 10 ft (3 m)—outran and devoured many kinds of prey.

Phorusrhacus Miocene, Argentina

Mammals take over

Warm-blooded mammals have existed for many millions of years. Dwarfed by dinosaurs for 165 million years, mammals survived the mass extinctions at the end of the Cretaceous period. Early mammals may have evaded dinosaur predators partly because they were small (rarely larger than rats) and appeared mainly at night. Dinosaurs had been a varied, successful group of animals, occupying many different habitats. After they became extinct, mammals took over. Two major groups of mammals are alive today, marsupials and placentals, and both give birth to live offspring. Marsupial young are immature at birth and develop further in the adult's pouch. Placental young are more advanced at birth, having been fed through the placenta inside the mother's womb. Although both groups are found as fossils in Cretaceous rocks, it was the placental mammals that became dominant on Earth.

MILK AND FUR
Fur coated, and able to convert food to energy quickly, mammals keep their body temperature constant. Newborns grow fast by feeding on nourishing milk from their mother's mammary glands. These specialized sweat glands are unique to mammals.

Foot

Pelvis

Fossil skeleton of *Megazostrodon*

Fur bristles have been fossilized

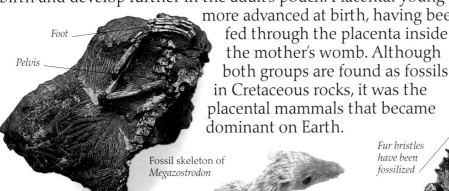

MINI MAMMAL
Looking like a shrew, *Megazostrodon* from South Africa belonged to a group of tiny mammals, the morganucodontids, of the Late Triassic and Early Jurassic periods. Covered with hair, *Megazostrodon* could maintain an efficient body temperature, unlike the sun-bathing reptiles.

Hair insulates body

Scaly plates on tail

Long tail helps balance

Model of *Megazostrodon*, one of the first mammals Late Triassic South Africa

Right hind foot

FIRST HERBIVORES
Rodentlike *Ptilodus* belonged to a mammal group called multituberculates (the first plant eaters). Surviving for over 100 million years, they became extinct in the Oligocene epoch. Multituberculates were named after their many-horned, grinding molar teeth. A ridged premolar provided a serrated slicing edge.

MAMMAL MOLARS
A few inches long and weighing about 0.7 oz (20 g), *Morganucodon* from the UK and China was one of the first mammals. It had a typically mammal-shaped lower jaw with a large lower jaw bone. Unlike similar-sized reptiles, this mammal had a large brain controlling movements and interpreting senses, including those from sensory hairs.

Thick coat of fur

Long prehensile tail

Reconstruction of squirrel-like *Ptilodus* Mid to Late Paleocene North America

Lower jaw of *Morganucodon* Late Triassic, UK and China

EOMAIA
Mouse-sized *Eomaia* is one of the most primitive members of Eutheria—a mammal group that includes the modern placental mammals and their fossil relatives. Its hands and feet were similar to modern climbing mammals, such as opossums. Tall, sharp points on its teeth suggest it was a predator of insects and other small animals.

Broken rear jaw where muscle attached

Double-rooted molar teeth with high, sharp-edged cusps for cutting up food

Feet with clawed toes

Cast of skull of *Uintatherium*, a horned ungulate (hoofed mammal) Eocene, North America

Pair of large horns at back of skull

Pair of smaller horns on forehead

Pair of nasal horns

Molar tooth

HORN-HEAD

One of the first large mammals, *Uintatherium* was the size of a rhinoceros. It lived 50 mya in North America. *Uintatherium* was a herbivore, using its broad, crested back teeth to slice up stems and leaves. Three pairs of horns adorned its skull; the largest pair at the rear and the smallest on top of the nose. The males also had a pair of large canine teeth; their elaborate skull ornaments may have helped to attract mates.

An adult *Uintatherium* with a youngster

FOSSIL FUR

At Germany's Messel quarry, oil shales have preserved a fantastic record of early mammals. During the Eocene epoch, this subtropical area was a freshwater lake filled with plant debris, clay, and dead animals. Horses, anteaters, primates, and other mammals have been found in the 47-million-year-old rocks. There was little oxygen at the bottom of the lake, so animals did not decay completely in the layers of sediment. Body outlines, stomach contents, and hair have been fossilized. *Pholidocercus* (a primitive hedgehog relative) still had its bristly fur coat.

Neck vertebra

Lower jaw

Insect-biting teeth

Fossil skeleton of *Pholidocercus*, an Eocene hedgehog relative from the Messel quarry in Germany

Front foot

Wing finger

Tail

BAT WINGS

Four-fingered struts, which once stretched thin wings, lie folded at the sides of Eocene *Palaeochiropteryx*, a fossil bat from Messel. *Palaeochiropteryx* was about 2.75 in (7 cm) long. It has been found with the fossilized remains of moths in its stomach. Bats are night fliers and rely on reflected sound signals to detect their prey, such as night-flying insects.

Head

Long tail

Rib cage

Toothlined jaw

HAIRY HEDGEHOG

Hedgehogs are insectivores, feeding on grubs, insects, and worms. *Macrocranion* is another fossil hedgehog relative, common among the finds at the Messel quarry site in Germany. Long-tailed, 8-in- (20-cm-) long *Macrocranion* was equipped with small, sharp teeth. This 47-million-year-old creature was like today's hedgehogs in many ways. It did not have a suit of spikes, but it was covered in tough hairs. They mark the fossil's body outline.

Mammal variety

MAMMALS ADAPTED TO A WIDE VARIETY of lifestyles. Over millions of years, the early shrewlike mammals evolved into ferocious hunters, bearlike browsers, and hoofed herbivores. Some mammals, such as whales, turned to a life in the sea. Others, such as bats, even managed to fly. Unlike reptiles, mammals did not rely on the Sun's heat for energy. As long as they had enough food, they were not tied to one climate or area. Mammal teeth provide us with clues to their diet. Carnivorous mammals have bladelike teeth for slicing and chewing meat; plant eaters have ridged, flat teeth that can grind up plants. There are few places where mammals have not found a home.

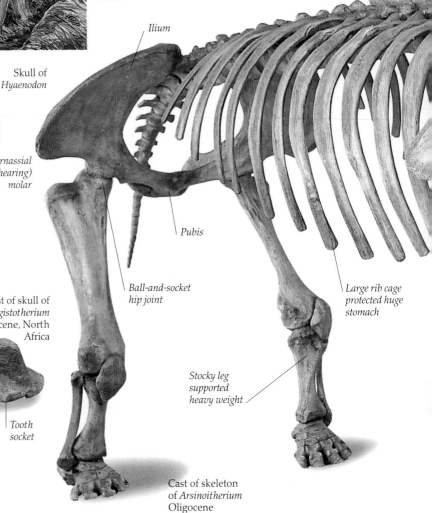

Top view of crest of *Prolibytherium* Early Miocene Libya

Attachment to skull

WINGED HORNS
The winged head plate of *Prolibytherium* (a small, slim, deerlike member of the giraffe family) looks little like the ossicones (head growths) of living giraffes. Giraffes were a diverse group of animals during the Miocene and Pliocene epochs in Africa and Asia.

Large-headed *Hyaenodon* standing by dead prey Early Tertiary, North America, Europe, and Africa

Ilium

Eye socket

Skull of *Hyaenodon*

Carnassial (shearing) molar

SMALL-BRAINED CARNIVORES
Now extinct, creodonts were the top carnivores in the early Tertiary period. *Hyaenodon* was a creodont that sometimes reached the size of today's living hyenas. Its carnassial teeth were adapted for shearing flesh, and its long canines were for stabbing. Creodonts had relatively large heads compared with modern carnivores—and remarkably small brains.

Pubis

Ball-and-socket hip joint

Large rib cage protected huge stomach

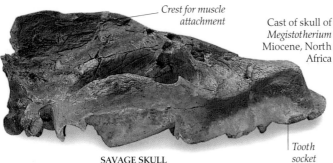

Crest for muscle attachment

Cast of skull of *Megistotherium* Miocene, North Africa

Stocky leg supported heavy weight

SAVAGE SKULL
Megistotherium was an enormous creodont that lived about 20 mya in what is now the Sahara Desert. *Megistotherium's* skull was 26 in (65 cm) long, twice the size of a lion's skull. The wide cheekbones and high-crested skull show that *Megistotherium* had enormous muscles to power its savage bite.

Tooth socket

Cast of skeleton of *Arsinoitherium* Oligocene Egypt

EARLY WHALE
Early whale *Basilosaurus* had a long body and small head. Front limbs were modified for swimming; rear limbs had nearly disappeared. The long snout had nostrils on its upper surface. Later whales breathed through special nostrils at the top of the head.

Model of 66-ft- (20-m-) long *Basilosaurus* Eocene, Atlantic coast of the US

Front limb was a flipper

Small trace of rear limb

Long tail

Eye socket

Front ossicone (head growth)

Nasal bone

Short-necked *Sivatherium* looked more like a giant elk than a giraffe

Skull of *Sivatherium giganteum*, Pliocene, India

TOUCHY NOSE
Sivatherium was a gigantic giraffid that lived in India and Africa during the Pliocene epoch. Only the front pair of ossicones are preserved in this fossil skull; a larger, heavier pair flared out from the back of the head. The strangely shaped nose bones suggest that *Sivatherium* may have had a prehensile (grasping) nose, as found in living tapirs.

Carnassial tooth

BEAR DOG
Bear dogs, the amphicyonids, were an important group of carnivore mammals ranging from the late Eocene to the Pliocene epochs. *Daphoenus* was one of the smaller amphicyonids, with a length of 3 ft (1 m). Many amphicyonids were large, stocky animals with bearlike bodies and doglike skulls.

Neural spine on vertebra

Strong neck vertebra

Skull of *Daphoenus* Oligocene, US

Movable joint in neck

A pair of long-tailed, lightly built *Daphoenus* bear dogs on the prowl for prey

Small horn over eyebrow

Deep-set eye socket

Bony horn with furrows left by blood vessels

POINTED HEAD
Horns of bone rather than tightly packed hair distinguish *Arsinoitherium* from living rhinoceroses. From the Oligocene epoch of Egypt, *Arsinoitherium* also differed from rhinos in having a complete set of incisor teeth. The molar teeth had large, crescent-shaped cutting edges, a feature found today in mammals whose diet consists mainly of leaves. Five fat toes on the end of each short, stocky limb carried its vast weight. *Arsinoitherium* belonged to a group of mammals called embrithopods, which became extinct in the Oligocene epoch.

Broad, chisel-edged molar for grinding plant food

Blocky, five-toed foot held up massive body

Nostril

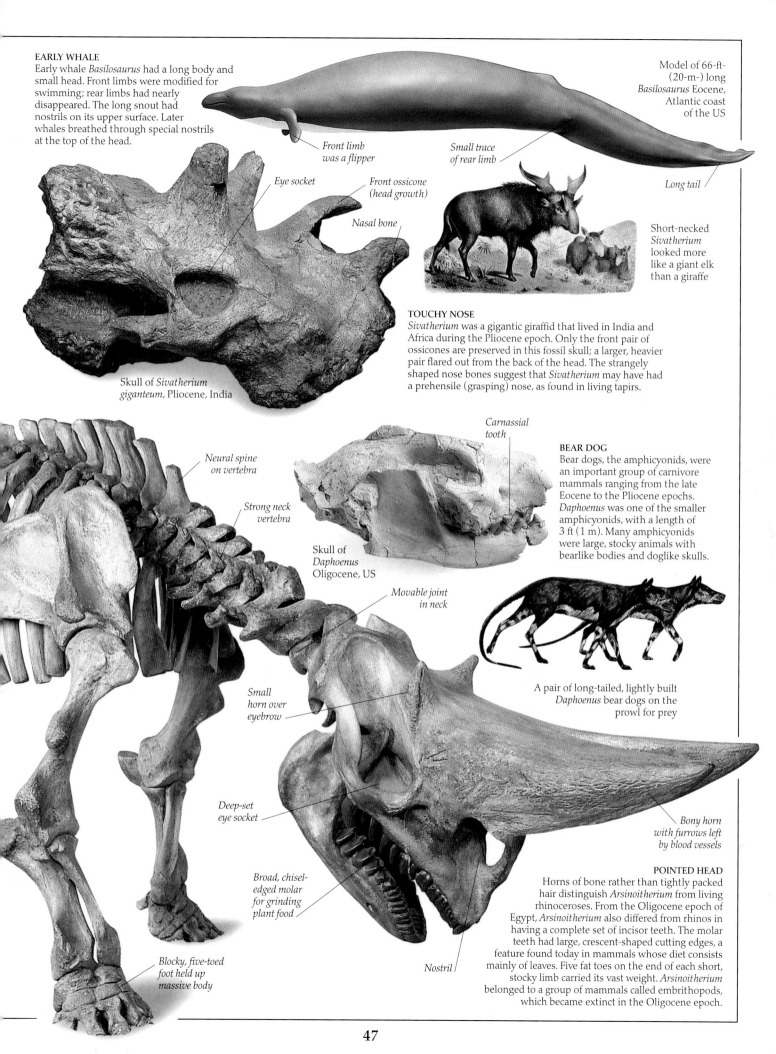

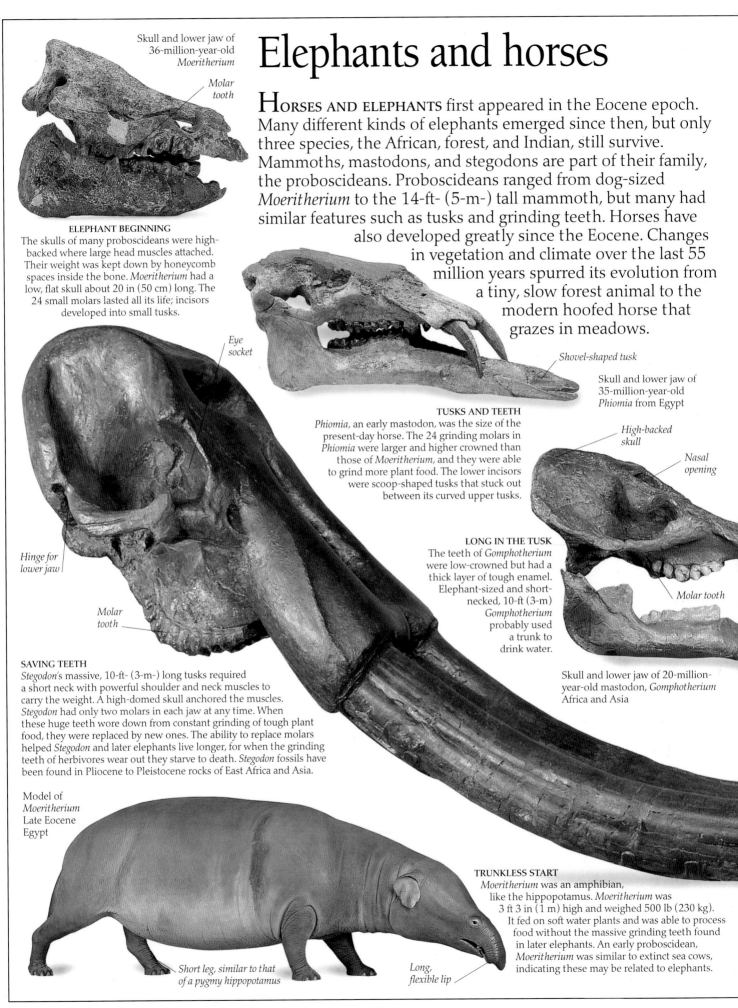

Elephants and horses

HORSES AND ELEPHANTS first appeared in the Eocene epoch. Many different kinds of elephants emerged since then, but only three species, the African, forest, and Indian, still survive. Mammoths, mastodons, and stegodons are part of their family, the proboscideans. Proboscideans ranged from dog-sized *Moeritherium* to the 14-ft- (5-m-) tall mammoth, but many had similar features such as tusks and grinding teeth. Horses have also developed greatly since the Eocene. Changes in vegetation and climate over the last 55 million years spurred its evolution from a tiny, slow forest animal to the modern hoofed horse that grazes in meadows.

Skull and lower jaw of 36-million-year-old Moeritherium

Molar tooth

ELEPHANT BEGINNING
The skulls of many proboscideans were high-backed where large head muscles attached. Their weight was kept down by honeycomb spaces inside the bone. *Moeritherium* had a low, flat skull about 20 in (50 cm) long. The 24 small molars lasted all its life; incisors developed into small tusks.

Eye socket

Shovel-shaped tusk

Skull and lower jaw of 35-million-year-old Phiomia from Egypt

TUSKS AND TEETH
Phiomia, an early mastodon, was the size of the present-day horse. The 24 grinding molars in *Phiomia* were larger and higher crowned than those of *Moeritherium*, and they were able to grind more plant food. The lower incisors were scoop-shaped tusks that stuck out between its curved upper tusks.

High-backed skull

Nasal opening

LONG IN THE TUSK
The teeth of *Gomphotherium* were low-crowned but had a thick layer of tough enamel. Elephant-sized and short-necked, 10-ft (3-m) *Gomphotherium* probably used a trunk to drink water.

Molar tooth

Hinge for lower jaw

Molar tooth

SAVING TEETH
Stegodon's massive, 10-ft- (3-m-) long tusks required a short neck with powerful shoulder and neck muscles to carry the weight. A high-domed skull anchored the muscles. *Stegodon* had only two molars in each jaw at any time. When these huge teeth wore down from constant grinding of tough plant food, they were replaced by new ones. The ability to replace molars helped *Stegodon* and later elephants live longer, for when the grinding teeth of herbivores wear out they starve to death. *Stegodon* fossils have been found in Pliocene to Pleistocene rocks of East Africa and Asia.

Skull and lower jaw of 20-million-year-old mastodon, Gomphotherium Africa and Asia

Model of Moeritherium Late Eocene Egypt

Short leg, similar to that of a pygmy hippopotamus

Long, flexible lip

TRUNKLESS START
Moeritherium was an amphibian, like the hippopotamus. *Moeritherium* was 3 ft 3 in (1 m) high and weighed 500 lb (230 kg). It fed on soft water plants and was able to process food without the massive grinding teeth found in later elephants. An early proboscidean, *Moeritherium* was similar to extinct sea cows, indicating these may be related to elephants.

48

Hooves and teeth

Horses have gone through their own distinct set of changes since they first appeared in the Eocene forests of 55 mya. Smaller than a domestic cat, the first horse, *Hyracotherium*, was a browser, feeding on seeds, fruit, and young leaves. It was not a fast animal, but padded on four-toed feet around forests. Over the next 55 million years, horses developed longer teeth to deal with tough, abrasive grasses.

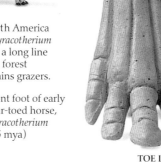

FIRST HORSE
Inhabiting North America and Europe, *Hyracotherium* was the first in a long line of horses, from forest browsers to plains grazers.

Front foot of early four-toed horse, *Hyracotherium* (55 mya)

TOE LOSS
In the progression to fewer toes, toe three became larger and longer until it became as broad as the horse's leg. Side toes were reduced and eventually lost in modern horses. Three-toed *Hipparion* placed most of its weight on its large middle toe. It probably managed a running walk of up to 9 mph (15 kph).

THREE-TOED HORSE
Three-toed *Merychippus* marked a major step in horse evolution. It was the first of the grazing horses and lived about 20 mya in North America.

Left hind foot of three-toed *Hipparion*, which lived from 23 mya in Europe, Asia, Africa, and North America

Feet, with fewer toes, geared to fast running on open plains over 55 million years

Low-crowned molar

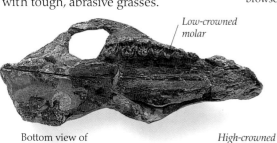

Bottom view of *Hyracotherium* skull

High-crowned tooth

Incisor

Bottom view of *Hipparion* skull

GRASS GRINDERS
During the early history of the horse, changes in climate reduced forests, and about 23 mya, grass plains spread over wide areas. Horses, such as *Hipparion*, adapted to a grazing way of life. They developed long, heavily ridged teeth. The ridges on the grinding surfaces were made of hard, tough tooth enamel. Like coarse files, the ridged tooth rows could grind the tough cellulose of grass plants.

Tusks of Stegodon were 10 ft (3 m) long

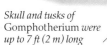

Skull and tusks of Gomphotherium were up to 7 ft (2 m) long

Skull and tusks of five-million-year-old *Stegodon ganesa* from India

TODAY'S ELEPHANTS
Elephants related to those living today first appeared about 7 mya. Today's elephants have only one large tooth in each jaw at a time. The back teeth slowly grow forward as the teeth in front wear down. New teeth replace old ones throughout life. Elephants can weigh close to 12 tons (11 metric tons) and must eat an enormous amount each day to survive.

SHORT TUSKS
Short-trunked *Phiomia* lived in North Africa about 32 mya. No more than 7 ft (2 m) tall, *Phiomia* was clearly elephant-like although its trunk, tusks, and body were still small. Cusped teeth had to grind through large volumes of plant food, wearing down to a flat grinding surface as they became older.

Short tusk used for rooting up plants

Model of *Phiomia* Early Oligocene, Egypt

Mammal islands

Engraving of *Diprotodon* from Australia

WHEN PANGAEA, the Mesozoic supercontinent, began to break up in the Jurassic period, each rift and seaway was an effective barrier to some groups of animals. South America and Australia became huge continental islands separated by sea barriers from other lands, and their mammal populations developed in isolation. South America and North America broke apart about 55 mya, at a time when marsupial (pouched) mammals were as widespread as placentals. For more than 50 million years, South America developed its own distinct marsupial and placental animal population, cut off from the rest of the world. About 3 mya, this mammal isolation ended when a bridge of land (the Isthmus of Panama) developed, providing a two-way migration route between North and South America. It is likely that the marsupials of Australia had come from Antarctica when it was much warmer than it is today. Australia broke away about 35 mya, and its mammal isolation has been more complete than that of the Americas.

PLEISTOCENE SCENE
Pleistocene Australia was a land of wondrous marsupial animals. Some became extinct only recently. Koalas, kangaroos, and the strangely primitive spiky echidna, an egg-laying mammal (bottom right), have survived to the present. However, wombatlike *Diprotodon*, lionlike *Thylacoleo*, and wolflike *Thylacinus* have become extinct, although the latter did so only recently.

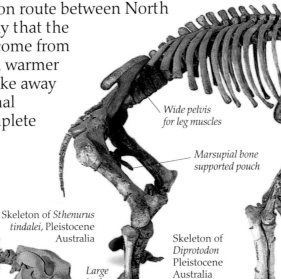

High nasal bone

Attachment area for neck muscles

Flat tooth for grinding *Curved incisor*

Wide pelvis for leg muscles

Marsupial bone supported pouch

Pelvis

Marsupial bone

Skeleton of *Sthenurus tindalei*, Pleistocene Australia

Large heel

Skeleton of *Diprotodon* Pleistocene Australia

Flat foot

Fossil skeleton of *Thylacoleo* Pleistocene Australia

Single long middle toe

Long-fingered hand

OUTSIZE AUSTRALIAN
An outsize marsupial, *Diprotodon* lived during the Pleistocene period of Australia. About 10 ft (3 m) long, *Diprotodon* was one of the largest plant-eating marsupials around. It had broad, plant-grinding molar teeth and huge incisors, like those of wombats. Short-limbed, stocky *Diprotodon* may have been still alive when the Aboriginals first inhabited Australia.

HOOFED HOPPER
Fast-moving hoppers, kangaroos may be up to 7 ft (2 m) tall, but some early kangaroos must have been taller than 10 ft (3 m) when alive. Short-jawed *Sthenurus* was a large Pliocene kangaroo, but unlike other kangaroos, its large rear foot had a single toe that ended in a hoof-shaped bone. It had a modified shoulder blade that helped it reach high above its head to eat young leaves at the tips of branches.

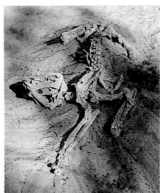

MAMMAL MIMIC
Wolflike *Thylacinus* was not the only mammal mimic. Marsupial *Thylacoleo* looked like a lion with its sharp, stabbing, and tearing incisor teeth and its slicing carnassial back teeth. *Thylacoleo* hunted Australia's Pleistocene marsupial herbivores, such as *Diprotodon* and kangaroos.

Distinctive stripes on back and tail

Reconstruction of *Thylacinus*, the "Tasmanian wolf" from the Miocene period of Australia; it only recently became extinct

TASMANIAN WOLF
Some marsupials were fearsome carnivores. *Thylacinus*, although similar in general appearance to the placental wolf of the Northern Hemisphere, was definitely a marsupial. The body shape and skulls are very much alike, and *Thylacinus* probably lived the same kind of pack-hunting life as its unrelated northern double. Known as the "Tasmanian wolf," *Thylacinus* became extinct in 1936.

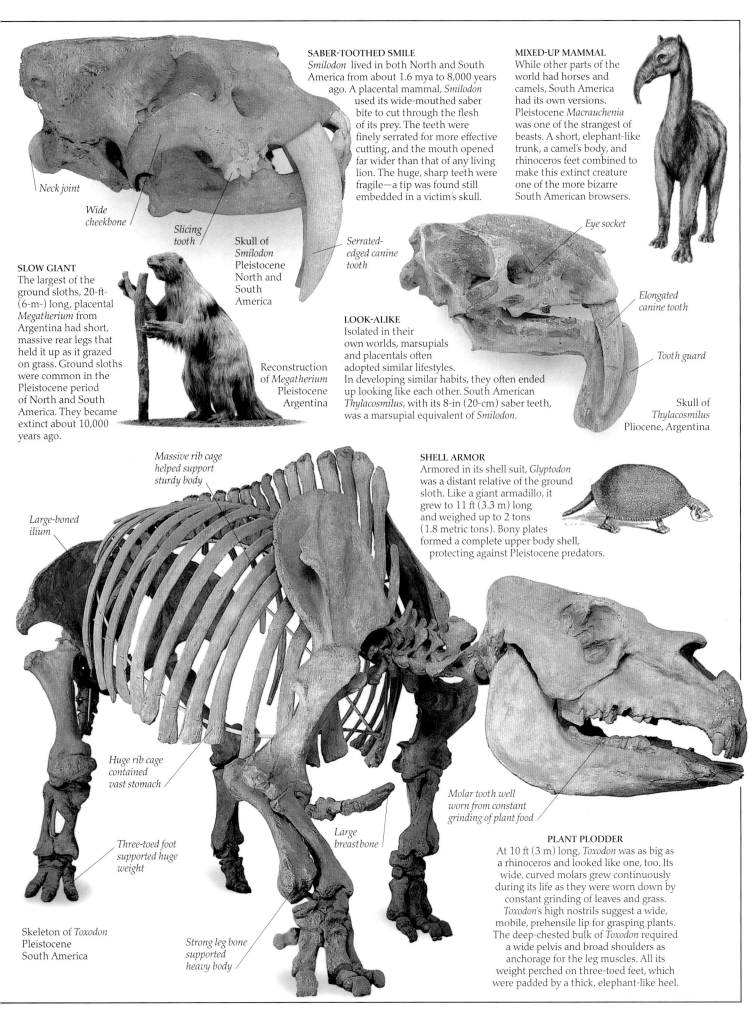

SABER-TOOTHED SMILE
Smilodon lived in both North and South America from about 1.6 mya to 8,000 years ago. A placental mammal, *Smilodon* used its wide-mouthed saber bite to cut through the flesh of its prey. The teeth were finely serrated for more effective cutting, and the mouth opened far wider than that of any living lion. The huge, sharp teeth were fragile—a tip was found still embedded in a victim's skull.

Neck joint

Wide cheekbone

Slicing tooth

Skull of *Smilodon* Pleistocene North and South America

Serrated-edged canine tooth

MIXED-UP MAMMAL
While other parts of the world had horses and camels, South America had its own versions. Pleistocene *Macrauchenia* was one of the strangest of beasts. A short, elephant-like trunk, a camel's body, and rhinoceros feet combined to make this extinct creature one of the more bizarre South American browsers.

Eye socket

Elongated canine tooth

Tooth guard

Skull of *Thylacosmilus* Pliocene, Argentina

SLOW GIANT
The largest of the ground sloths, 20-ft- (6-m-) long, placental *Megatherium* from Argentina had short, massive rear legs that held it up as it grazed on grass. Ground sloths were common in the Pleistocene period of North and South America. They became extinct about 10,000 years ago.

Reconstruction of *Megatherium* Pleistocene Argentina

LOOK-ALIKE
Isolated in their own worlds, marsupials and placentals often adopted similar lifestyles. In developing similar habits, they often ended up looking like each other. South American *Thylacosmilus*, with its 8-in (20-cm) saber teeth, was a marsupial equivalent of *Smilodon*.

SHELL ARMOR
Armored in its shell suit, *Glyptodon* was a distant relative of the ground sloth. Like a giant armadillo, it grew to 11 ft (3.3 m) long and weighed up to 2 tons (1.8 metric tons). Bony plates formed a complete upper body shell, protecting against Pleistocene predators.

Massive rib cage helped support sturdy body

Large-boned ilium

Huge rib cage contained vast stomach

Three-toed foot supported huge weight

Skeleton of *Toxodon* Pleistocene South America

Strong leg bone supported heavy body

Large breastbone

Molar tooth well worn from constant grinding of plant food

PLANT PLODDER
At 10 ft (3 m) long, *Toxodon* was as big as a rhinoceros and looked like one, too. Its wide, curved molars grew continuously during its life as they were worn down by constant grinding of leaves and grass. *Toxodon*'s high nostrils suggest a wide, mobile, prehensile lip for grasping plants. The deep-chested bulk of *Toxodon* required a wide pelvis and broad shoulders as anchorage for the leg muscles. All its weight perched on three-toed feet, which were padded by a thick, elephant-like heel.

Birth and growth

LIFE HAS SURVIVED ON EARTH for more than 3 billion years. From the beginning, it found a way to reproduce itself. Cyanobacteria (blue-green algae) simply divided their cells in two, each exactly like the other. Later, sexual reproduction increased the variety of life. Male and female cells combined to produce an offspring different from both parents, increasing the chances of further change. Some animals, such as fish and amphibians, laid their fragile eggs in water, but the first reptile produced a new, amniotic egg. Protected by a tough, waterproof eggshell, the embryo developed in its own watery environment enclosed within the amnion (embryo sac). Reptiles were freed up to live on land, though some developed as marine animals, giving birth at sea. Mammals, which also have amniotic eggs, gave them further protection by keeping the eggs and developing young inside their bodies until birth.

TADPOLE TALE
Amphibian eggs are covered in a thick layer of protective albumen (the white of the egg). In water, the albumen becomes sticky, holding the eggs together as a mass. The frogs then pass through a tadpole stage. This rare fossil never got any further.

Coral released egg into water

BRANCHING OUT
Set in their stony skeletons, the coral polyps produce side branches by building. Each new branch adds to the coral colony. At intervals, the polyps also eject male and female cells, which combine to produce free-swimming coral animals. Survivors settle and grow into new coral colonies.

Thecosmilia trichotoma (colony of coral with separate branches), Late Jurassic Germany

Rejuvenating corallite branch increases colony

Red shows one embryo (of six) that died with adult female

Maiasaura *eggs were laid in a scooped-out hollow in sand and covered with vegetation, as shown in this model*

Stenopterygius quadriscissus
Early Jurassic, Germany

FOSSIL BIRTH
The fish-shaped ichthyosaurs descended from land reptiles that had returned to the sea. They did not lay eggs but gave birth to live young in the water. Ichthyosaur fossils have been found with the young still inside the body. This *Stenopterygius* probably died from some difficulty during birth.

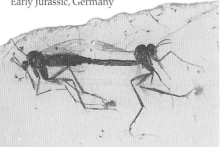

INSECT TRAP
Trapped in the sticky resin of a tree, these mating flies were fossilized in golden amber. At some stage, insects "invented" metamorphosis, growth by changing form. Instead of going from an egg to a small version of an adult that grows in size, insects change from egg to larva (like a caterpillar) to pupa to adult.

Aepyornis lived during the Pleistocene epoch on Madagascar and laid its eggs in sand dunes

RECORD STORE

Like many other mollusks, an ammonoid records the history of its growth in its coiled shell, called an ammonite. At the center of the coil is the protoconch (first small shell cover). As it grew outward, the tentacled ammonoid occupied a series of chambers. Each chamber, larger than the previous one, was a new stage in its growth. The chambers, coiling out from the center, were filled with gas and kept the animal buoyant in the sea.

ELEPHANT BIRD EGG

It is not surprising that giant birds should lay giant eggs. The 10-ft- (3-m-) tall, flightless *Aepyornis* holds the record. Weighing about 1,000 lb (450 kg), *Aepyornis* laid eggs 170 times larger than those of hens. However, larger eggs need thicker shells, which limits their size. If the shell was too thick, the chick could not break out.

PALM FRUIT

Plants developed many ways to spread their seeds. When a tasty fruit was eaten by an animal, the tough seeds survived intact and were excreted, often far from their source. The coconut-like fruit of *Nipa*, a stemless palm, enclosed seeds up to 3 in (8 cm) long. The fruit was probably either carried away by water or split open in *Nipa*'s tropical habitat.

Woody outer layer enclosed large seeds in fibrous inner layer

Fruit of *Nipa burtinii*, Mid Eocene, Belgium

Oxynoticeras oxynotum, Early Jurassic, UK

Chamber filled with crystals during fossilization

DINOSAUR PLAYPEN

The first complete and well-preserved eggs were first recognized in 1922, when fossilized nests of *Oviraptor* were discovered in the Gobi Desert. Since then, many more dinosaur eggs have been discovered. Some of the most exciting discoveries were made in Montana, where nesting sites of *Maiasaura* were found in 1978. *Maiasaura* ("good mother lizard") not only laid its eggs in scooped-out nests but perhaps also cared for the young, 14-in (36-cm) hatchlings, until they were large enough to look after themselves.

Apes and ancestors

We humans are unique in our upright walk, spoken language, advanced use of tools and fire, and level of intelligence. However, evidence from our body shape points to the sociable, tool-using chimpanzees as our closest living relatives. Although it may offend some people, scientific evidence places humans, gorillas, and chimpanzees in the same group—Hominoidea. On a wider scale, humans are members of the Primates group, along with 200 other species of monkeys, apes, and prosimians (a group of animals including lemurs and bush babies). This does not mean that gorillas and chimpanzees were our ancestors but that at some point in the past, humans and apes had a common ancestor. Since then, apes have developed along their own line and humans along another. Fossils of primates help pinpoint the junctions where lines branched, where groups split and headed off in new and different directions.

No eyebrow ridge

Shallow eye socket

AEGYPTOPITHECUS
Discovered in the desert of Fayum in Egypt, tree-living *Aegyptopithecus* lived about 32 mya when the area was a tropical rainforest. Although monkeylike, this small primate was distinct from both apes and monkeys and may have been very similar to the common ancestor of both.

PROCONSUL
Named in 1933, *Proconsul africanus* combined the skeletal features of modern monkeys and apes. A representative of the earliest apes, *Proconsul* had the hands, arms, and long body of tree-swinging monkeys but it also had the skull, shoulders, and elbows of knuckle-walking apes. There were several species of *Proconsul* of very different sizes. These first apes of 20 mya fed in the woods and forests of what is now Kenya.

Partial skull of *Sivapithecus indicus* (10.5–8 mya) Pakistan

Long face curves down to projecting mouth

Thickened ridge on lower side of jaw

Small lateral incisor, as in today's orangutan

ORANGUTAN ANCESTOR
Making links between living hominoids and fossils is difficult. It is only the orangutan that can be linked reasonably well to an early ape. *Sivapithecus*, found in Miocene rocks of 13–8 mya, displays the long face, projecting mouth, and flattened cheeks that help identify this orangutan line of apes. More distant from humans than the gorilla and chimpanzee, *Sivapithecus* was an early branch off the line that went on to produce the African apes and humans. Named after the Indian god Siva and found in India, Pakistan, and Turkey, *Sivapithecus* is the earliest hominoid outside Africa.

Flat, thick tooth enamel similar to that of an orangutan

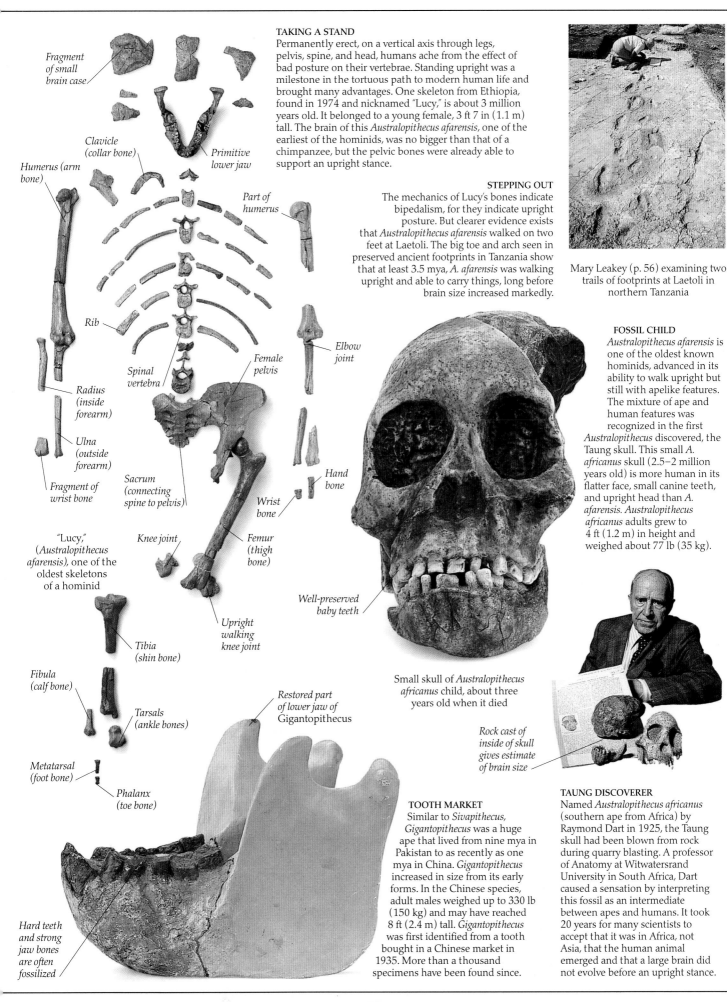

Fragment of small brain case

Clavicle (collar bone)

Primitive lower jaw

Humerus (arm bone)

Part of humerus

Rib

Elbow joint

Spinal vertebra

Female pelvis

Radius (inside forearm)

Ulna (outside forearm)

Hand bone

Fragment of wrist bone

Sacrum (connecting spine to pelvis)

Wrist bone

"Lucy," (Australopithecus afarensis), one of the oldest skeletons of a hominid

Knee joint

Femur (thigh bone)

Upright walking knee joint

Tibia (shin bone)

Fibula (calf bone)

Tarsals (ankle bones)

Metatarsal (foot bone)

Phalanx (toe bone)

Restored part of lower jaw of Gigantopithecus

Hard teeth and strong jaw bones are often fossilized

Well-preserved baby teeth

Small skull of Australopithecus africanus child, about three years old when it died

Rock cast of inside of skull gives estimate of brain size

TAKING A STAND

Permanently erect, on a vertical axis through legs, pelvis, spine, and head, humans ache from the effect of bad posture on their vertebrae. Standing upright was a milestone in the tortuous path to modern human life and brought many advantages. One skeleton from Ethiopia, found in 1974 and nicknamed "Lucy," is about 3 million years old. It belonged to a young female, 3 ft 7 in (1.1 m) tall. The brain of this *Australopithecus afarensis*, one of the earliest of the hominids, was no bigger than that of a chimpanzee, but the pelvic bones were already able to support an upright stance.

STEPPING OUT

The mechanics of Lucy's bones indicate bipedalism, for they indicate upright posture. But clearer evidence exists that *Australopithecus afarensis* walked on two feet at Laetoli. The big toe and arch seen in preserved ancient footprints in Tanzania show that at least 3.5 mya, *A. afarensis* was walking upright and able to carry things, long before brain size increased markedly.

Mary Leakey (p. 56) examining two trails of footprints at Laetoli in northern Tanzania

FOSSIL CHILD

Australopithecus afarensis is one of the oldest known hominids, advanced in its ability to walk upright but still with apelike features. The mixture of ape and human features was recognized in the first *Australopithecus* discovered, the Taung skull. This small *A. africanus* skull (2.5–2 million years old) is more human in its flatter face, small canine teeth, and upright head than *A. afarensis*. *Australopithecus africanus* adults grew to 4 ft (1.2 m) in height and weighed about 77 lb (35 kg).

TOOTH MARKET

Similar to *Sivapithecus*, *Gigantopithecus* was a huge ape that lived from nine mya in Pakistan to as recently as one mya in China. *Gigantopithecus* increased in size from its early forms. In the Chinese species, adult males weighed up to 330 lb (150 kg) and may have reached 8 ft (2.4 m) tall. *Gigantopithecus* was first identified from a tooth bought in a Chinese market in 1935. More than a thousand specimens have been found since.

TAUNG DISCOVERER

Named *Australopithecus africanus* (southern ape from Africa) by Raymond Dart in 1925, the Taung skull had been blown from rock during quarry blasting. A professor of Anatomy at Witwatersrand University in South Africa, Dart caused a sensation by interpreting this fossil as an intermediate between apes and humans. It took 20 years for many scientists to accept that it was in Africa, not Asia, that the human animal emerged and that a large brain did not evolve before an upright stance.

Early humans

THE ORIGIN OF MODERN HUMANS (*Homo sapiens*) is a subject of serious debate among scientists. The arguments are heated because discoveries of fossil humans are relatively rare, many having been made only since the early 1960s. Every detail revealed is important, as changes in humans have occurred in a relatively short time. Modern humans may have appeared as recently as 195,000 years ago. In some places, they lived alongside Neanderthals for over 40,000 years. Neanderthals changed little, remaining a distinct people until they died out about 30,000 years ago. Modern humans seem to have appeared first in Africa and then spread through the world.

OLDUVAI GORGE
In Tanzania's Serengeti Plain, Olduvai Gorge with its layers of volcanic and sedimentary rock (2–0.1 mya) is the site where the first-known human, *Homo habilis*, and the later *Homo erectus* were discovered. British paleontologists Louis Leakey (1903–72) and his wife, Mary (1913–36), discovered the skull of a 1.8-million-year-old hominid in 1964.

Body completely covered with hair

Cranium of *Homo habilis*

Teeth like those of A. africanus

HANDY HUMAN
The discovery of *Homo habilis* at Olduvai and at other African sites prompted a debate about its *Australopithecus*-like flat-sided face and tree-climbing ability compared with their more human-sized brain capacity and precise gripping hand.

Stone hammer for smashing bones or shaping tools

TOOL MAKER
Some scientists believe that the differences between *Australopithecus africanus* (pp. 54–55) and later *Homo erectus* are so small that intermediate *H. habilis* remains are really *A. africanus* or *H. erectus*. One robust kind of *Australopithecus* lived at Olduvai at the same time as *H. habilis*. The probable presence of larger-brained *H. habilis* is seen in the rough stone tools for scraping, cutting, and chopping found at Olduvai. The oldest tools of these kind (2.5 mya) come from sites farther north in Ethiopia. *H. habilis* could have used them to cut meat and break open bones and hard fruit.

Model of *Homo habilis*, an upright walker with a large brain

Homo habilis may have had a tool kit of differently shaped stone tools

Cranium of *Homo erectus* from Koobi Fora in northern Kenya

Wide-set eyes

Broad-based skull

Low skull cap with jutting brow ridge

Cranium of *Homo neanderthalensis* from Neander Valley in Germany

Brain as large as modern human's

Heavy, projecting brow ridge

Skull of male Neanderthal found at La Ferrassie Cave

Low forehead

Large, protruding teeth

THICK SKULL
Discovered in 1856, the thick skull cap and some limb bones were the first Neanderthal fossils to be recognized. Named after the site of their discovery, the Neander Valley near Dusseldorf in Germany, Neanderthals probably appeared over 200,000 years ago. They are well known from remains between 35,000 and 70,000 years old.

LARGE BRAIN
Neanderthals had a flat-topped, low skull with prominent bony eyebrow ridges. Their large face was marked by a huge nose, receding cheekbones, and large, projecting teeth. The lower jaw often had no bony chin, as in this specimen from La Ferrassie Cave in southwest France. Usually, a Neanderthal brain was larger (88 cu in, 1,450 cu cm) than a modern human's, but this 50,000-year-old male skull had a brain capacity of 98 cu in (1,600 cu cm). Neanderthals lived alongside modern humans in some places but remained distinct. They are a dead end in the human story.

UPRIGHT HUMANS
Fossils of *Homo erectus* (upright human) were first found in Indonesia in 1890. Until the discovery of other fossils in Africa in 1954, *H. erectus* was only known from Indonesia and China. From the Leakeys' find in the 1960s, we now know that *H. erectus* first appeared in East Africa 1.8 mya and spread into Asia by 1 mya. Larger brained than *H. habilis*, *H. erectus* flaked stones for handaxes and butchered meat.

Large lower jaw and teeth

Thick humerus (upper arm bone)

NEANDERTHAL PEOPLE
Neanderthals appeared over 200,000 years ago in Europe and western Asia. Stockily built, males were 5 ft 7 in (1.7 m) tall and females 5 ft 3 in (1.6 m). Neanderthals have a reputation for being stupid and primitive, but they were clever enough to survive in cold climates during ice ages. They made stone (but not antler or bone) tools.

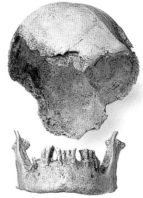

TWO GROUPS
In Australia, the oldest human remains (40,000–50,000 years old), from Lake Mungo, are of slim, lightly built people (above). Also present at the same time were people with heavier skulls. These two distinct groups may have been the result of more than one migration to this island continent.

BURIAL RITES
Neanderthals may have been the first people to bury their dead. At Kebara Cave on Mount Carmel in Israel 60,000 years ago, the large skeleton of a young man was deliberately buried without his skull. His massive jaw was covered up along with his skeleton after the flesh had rotted. Other Neanderthal burials may have been marked by flowers in the grave.

Cro-Magnon cranium

HUMAN APPEARANCE
In Europe 30,000 years ago, modern humans dominated the cold, unfriendly landscape. These Cro-Magnons, named after their rock shelter in France, wore animal hides, made fine bone harpoons and delicate stone tools, and built huts or lived in caves. They were distinct from the disappearing Neanderthals, both in their culture and in their tall, slim appearance.

Panthera spelaea
Pleistocene
Europe

Ice ages

OVER MANY THOUSANDS OF YEARS, the Earth's path around the Sun alters so that parts of the Earth's surface are closer to or farther from the Sun and become warmer or cooler. During cold periods, winter snow may stay into summer. A small drop in global temperature (as little as 4°F, 2°C), can disrupt the normal thawing of winter ice. Reflecting the Sun's rays, ice can lower the global temperature, and any volcanic dust thrown into the atmosphere can block the Sun and cool the Earth. Ice ages, with cold periods (glacials) that alternate with warm periods (interglacials), have been a recurring feature for at least 2 billion years. Over the past 1.6 million years, animal and plant life have had to deal with advancing and retreating ice sheets. Today, the Earth is in a warm, interglacial period.

NORTHERN LION
Lions live today only in Africa and India. In Europe, the cave lion (*Panthera spelaea*) died out 10,000 years ago. Its fossilized remains have been found in warm, interglacial deposits, where wide open grasslands let lions hunt for prey.

Hedera
(Ivy)

Small ear cuts loss of body heat

Enormous ivory tusk curved up and inward

MAMMOTH MONSTER
Of all ice age animals, the woolly mammoth, *Mammuthus primigenius*, is the most famous. About 10 ft (3 m) tall at the shoulders, mammoths had a long, shaggy coat of thick, dark hair and a layer of insulating fat. Great numbers of woolly mammoths ranged across the cold tundra regions of North America, Europe, and Asia. More than 500,000 tons (454,000 metric tons) of fossil tusks are estimated to be buried along 900 miles (1,500 km) of Siberian coastline. The tusks are collected for their ivory. Thought to have become extinct 10,000 years ago, recently found remains of smaller woolly mammoths show they were still alive 4,000 years ago.

PLANT THERMOMETER
Some plants thrive in warm climates, while others can survive much lower temperatures. In northern Europe, ivy needs an average winter monthly temperature higher than 29°F (-1.5°C) to thrive. The ice ages' warmer, interglacial periods can be identified by fossil ivy pollen from Pleistocene sediments.

DEEP FREEZE
Dima, a baby woolly mammoth, was just six months old when it died. Preserved in Arctic permafrost (permanently frozen soil), Dima remained frozen for 40,000 years until discovered by gold miners in 1977. Its carcass still had a coat of red hair.

Mollusk shell attached to root

Woolly mammoth tooth

DRY LAND
Dredged from the North Sea, this mammoth tooth with a mollusk shell stuck on its roots indicates a time when the seabed was exposed as dry land. Ice caps trapped vast quantities of water, and the sea-level fell by as much as 330 ft (100 m). Ice age mammals were able to cross land bridges from Alaska to Siberia, New Guinea to Australia, and the European mainland to Great Britain.

Thick, woolly underhair

Hair covered trunk to keep out cold

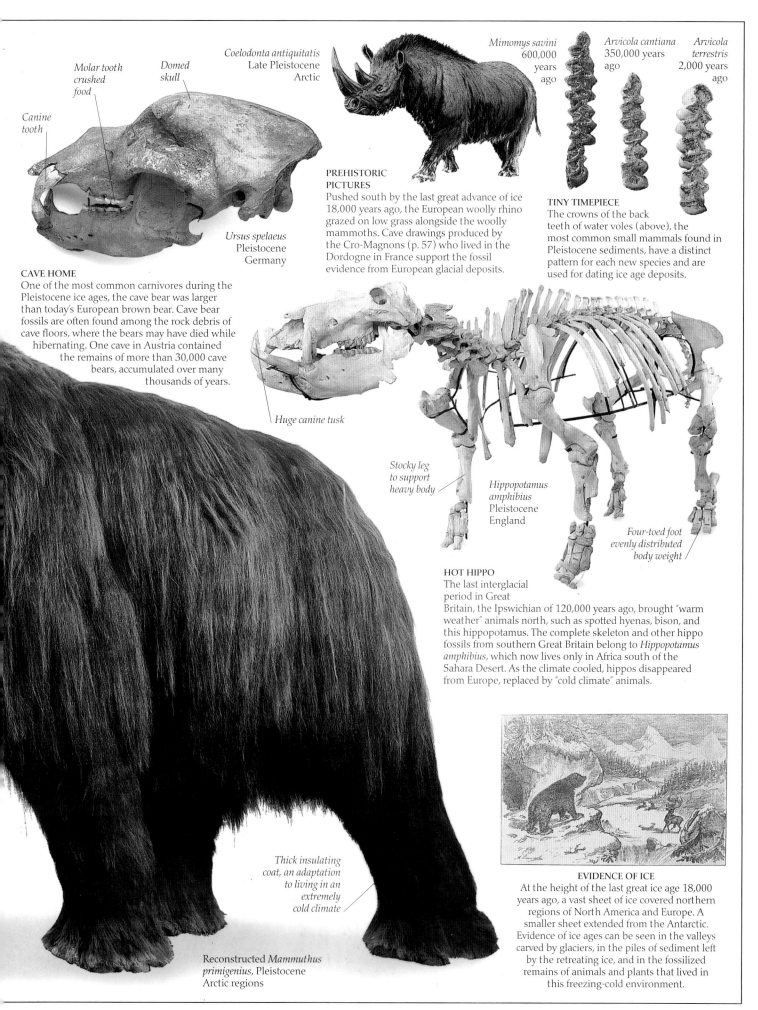

Molar tooth crushed food

Domed skull

Canine tooth

Coelodonta antiquitatis
Late Pleistocene
Arctic

Mimomys savini
600,000 years ago

Arvicola cantiana
350,000 years ago

Arvicola terrestris
2,000 years ago

Ursus spelaeus
Pleistocene
Germany

PREHISTORIC PICTURES
Pushed south by the last great advance of ice 18,000 years ago, the European woolly rhino grazed on low grass alongside the woolly mammoths. Cave drawings produced by the Cro-Magnons (p. 57) who lived in the Dordogne in France support the fossil evidence from European glacial deposits.

TINY TIMEPIECE
The crowns of the back teeth of water voles (above), the most common small mammals found in Pleistocene sediments, have a distinct pattern for each new species and are used for dating ice age deposits.

CAVE HOME
One of the most common carnivores during the Pleistocene ice ages, the cave bear was larger than today's European brown bear. Cave bear fossils are often found among the rock debris of cave floors, where the bears may have died while hibernating. One cave in Austria contained the remains of more than 30,000 cave bears, accumulated over many thousands of years.

Huge canine tusk

Stocky leg to support heavy body

Hippopotamus amphibius
Pleistocene
England

Four-toed foot evenly distributed body weight

HOT HIPPO
The last interglacial period in Great Britain, the Ipswichian of 120,000 years ago, brought "warm weather" animals north, such as spotted hyenas, bison, and this hippopotamus. The complete skeleton and other hippo fossils from southern Great Britain belong to *Hippopotamus amphibius*, which now lives only in Africa south of the Sahara Desert. As the climate cooled, hippos disappeared from Europe, replaced by "cold climate" animals.

Thick insulating coat, an adaptation to living in an extremely cold climate

Reconstructed *Mammuthus primigenius*, Pleistocene
Arctic regions

EVIDENCE OF ICE
At the height of the last great ice age 18,000 years ago, a vast sheet of ice covered northern regions of North America and Europe. A smaller sheet extended from the Antarctic. Evidence of ice ages can be seen in the valleys carved by glaciers, in the piles of sediment left by the retreating ice, and in the fossilized remains of animals and plants that lived in this freezing-cold environment.

Extinction

DEATH IS AS IMPORTANT as birth in the development of life. The extinction of one group of animals creates an opportunity for another group and, in a relatively short time, can completely change the direction of life. Mass extinctions have occurred several times in Earth's history. The largest extinction, at the end of the Permian period (251 mya), wiped out over half the marine families and two-thirds of the tetrapod animals on land. The main cause of the extinction of dinosaurs may have been an asteroid or a comet collision with Earth. The key lies in a layer of clay between rocks of the Cretaceous and Tertiary periods. Iridium, found in quantity only in meteorites, is so rich in this worldwide band of clay that, measured against the normal fallout from space, it could only have come from a massive meteorite. Hence, the debate on a wipe-out due to a hit by an asteroid or a comet is still on.

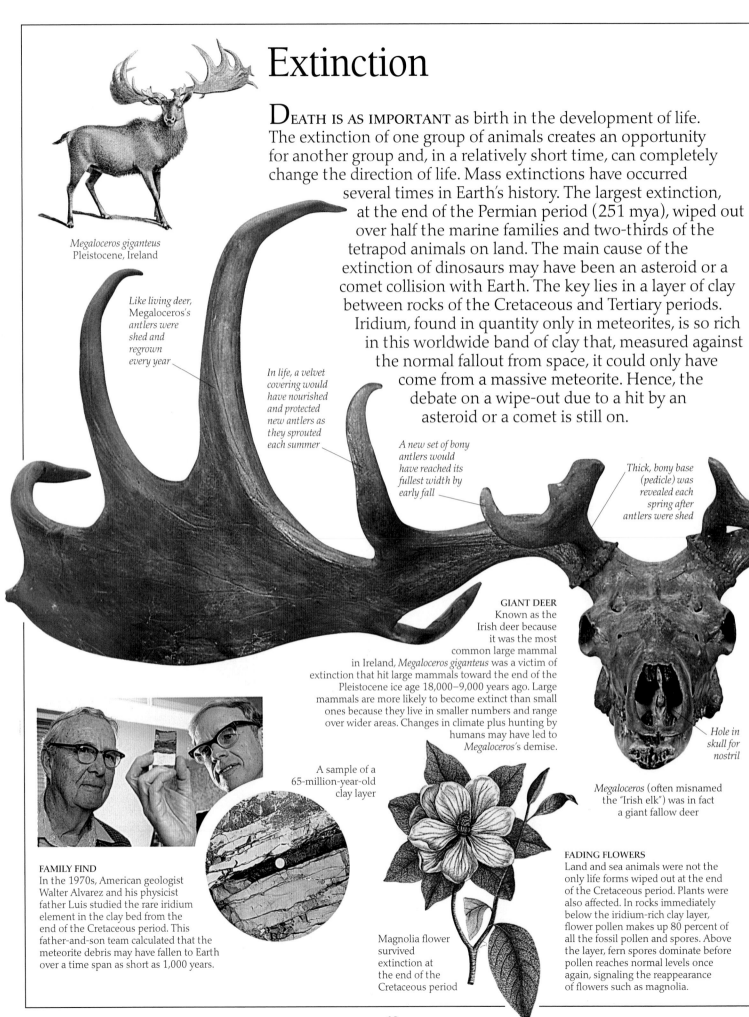

Megaloceros giganteus
Pleistocene, Ireland

Like living deer, Megaloceros's antlers were shed and regrown every year

In life, a velvet covering would have nourished and protected new antlers as they sprouted each summer

A new set of bony antlers would have reached its fullest width by early fall

Thick, bony base (pedicle) was revealed each spring after antlers were shed

GIANT DEER
Known as the Irish deer because it was the most common large mammal in Ireland, *Megaloceros giganteus* was a victim of extinction that hit large mammals toward the end of the Pleistocene ice age 18,000–9,000 years ago. Large mammals are more likely to become extinct than small ones because they live in smaller numbers and range over wider areas. Changes in climate plus hunting by humans may have led to *Megaloceros*'s demise.

Hole in skull for nostril

Megaloceros (often misnamed the "Irish elk") was in fact a giant fallow deer

FAMILY FIND
In the 1970s, American geologist Walter Alvarez and his physicist father Luis studied the rare iridium element in the clay bed from the end of the Cretaceous period. This father-and-son team calculated that the meteorite debris may have fallen to Earth over a time span as short as 1,000 years.

A sample of a 65-million-year-old clay layer

Magnolia flower survived extinction at the end of the Cretaceous period

FADING FLOWERS
Land and sea animals were not the only life forms wiped out at the end of the Cretaceous period. Plants were also affected. In rocks immediately below the iridium-rich clay layer, flower pollen makes up 80 percent of all the fossil pollen and spores. Above the layer, fern spores dominate before pollen reaches normal levels once again, signaling the reappearance of flowers such as magnolia.

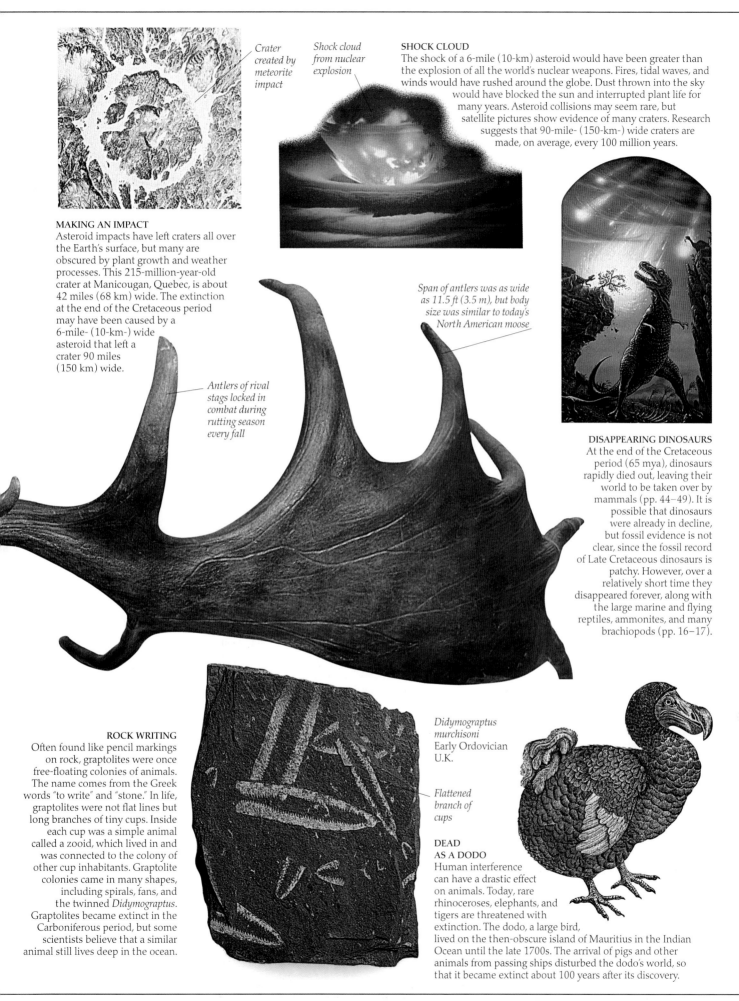

Crater created by meteorite impact

Shock cloud from nuclear explosion

SHOCK CLOUD

The shock of a 6-mile (10-km) asteroid would have been greater than the explosion of all the world's nuclear weapons. Fires, tidal waves, and winds would have rushed around the globe. Dust thrown into the sky would have blocked the sun and interrupted plant life for many years. Asteroid collisions may seem rare, but satellite pictures show evidence of many craters. Research suggests that 90-mile- (150-km-) wide craters are made, on average, every 100 million years.

MAKING AN IMPACT

Asteroid impacts have left craters all over the Earth's surface, but many are obscured by plant growth and weather processes. This 215-million-year-old crater at Manicougan, Quebec, is about 42 miles (68 km) wide. The extinction at the end of the Cretaceous period may have been caused by a 6-mile- (10-km-) wide asteroid that left a crater 90 miles (150 km) wide.

Span of antlers was as wide as 11.5 ft (3.5 m), but body size was similar to today's North American moose

Antlers of rival stags locked in combat during rutting season every fall

DISAPPEARING DINOSAURS

At the end of the Cretaceous period (65 mya), dinosaurs rapidly died out, leaving their world to be taken over by mammals (pp. 44–49). It is possible that dinosaurs were already in decline, but fossil evidence is not clear, since the fossil record of Late Cretaceous dinosaurs is patchy. However, over a relatively short time they disappeared forever, along with the large marine and flying reptiles, ammonites, and many brachiopods (pp. 16–17).

ROCK WRITING

Often found like pencil markings on rock, graptolites were once free-floating colonies of animals. The name comes from the Greek words "to write" and "stone." In life, graptolites were not flat lines but long branches of tiny cups. Inside each cup was a simple animal called a zooid, which lived in and was connected to the colony of other cup inhabitants. Graptolite colonies came in many shapes, including spirals, fans, and the twinned *Didymograptus*. Graptolites became extinct in the Carboniferous period, but some scientists believe that a similar animal still lives deep in the ocean.

Didymograptus murchisoni Early Ordovician U.K.

Flattened branch of cups

DEAD AS A DODO

Human interference can have a drastic effect on animals. Today, rare rhinoceroses, elephants, and tigers are threatened with extinction. The dodo, a large bird, lived on the then-obscure island of Mauritius in the Indian Ocean until the late 1700s. The arrival of pigs and other animals from passing ships disturbed the dodo's world, so that it became extinct about 100 years after its discovery.

Fossil finders

FOSSILS CAN BE FOUND in many places where rocks are exposed, such as quarries and coastlines. Collecting does not require much equipment; it is better to look among loose boulders than to hammer and chip at dangerous cliffs. At coastal edges, rising tides are a danger, and tide time tables must be consulted. Landowners must be asked for permission before fossil hunting begins. Some sites are so famous for their fossils that no collecting is allowed, thus preserving the treasures for everyone.

Modern geological map

Sculptor's hammer

Broad-bladed bolster (special chisel)

Geological hammer

FAKE FOSSILS
Rocks often have interesting and curious shapes that can be mistaken for the fossil remains of organisms. One important reason why museums collect and study fossil remains is to compare them with new finds. Museums also help identify fake fossils—stone or other material deliberately made to look like fossils. Some famous fakes have been produced, such as these sea creatures published in a book in Germany in 1726. Fake fossils are usually recognized eventually, but swindlers still try to sell them.

A collection of safety equipment and collecting tools for the young fossil finder

FOSSIL FOOTPRINTS
Some fossils, like footprints, cannot be removed from their enclosing rock. But a cast of the impression can be made in plaster and then removed. Footprints, as well as large fossil skeletons, can cover a wide area. A great deal of hard work may be needed to uncover a whole trackway, such as these dinosaur footprints.

FIELD TOOLS
Specially made geological hammers are useful for breaking open lumps of rock. Sculptor's hammers can be used with large chisels to split flat slabs of rock that contain fossils.

Small rocks inset with brachiopods

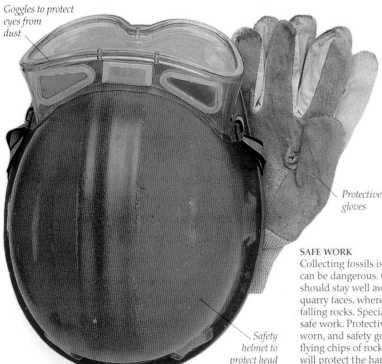

Goggles to protect eyes from dust

Protective gloves

Safety helmet to protect head from falling rocks

SAFE WORK
Collecting fossils is fun but it can be dangerous. Collectors should stay well away from cliff and quarry faces, where there is always a risk of falling rocks. Special clothing is needed for safe work. Protective safety helmets must be worn, and safety goggles will protect eyes from flying chips of rock when hammering. Tough gloves will protect the hands from sharp edges. Cloth collecting bags are useful for carrying fossil finds.

Collecting bag for storing fossil finds

ROCK LAYOUT

Only certain kinds of rocks contain fossils, and it helps to know where these rocks are. Just as there are maps showing towns, mountains, and rivers, geologists have produced maps that show where different rock layers can be found on the Earth's surface. These can be studied to discover where fossils might be found.

Pneumatic engraving tool can remove rock quickly

Diamond-edged dental wheel for cutting into the rock

A small hammer and chisel delicately remove rock

PREPARING FOSSILS

Sometimes fossils are collected still embedded in rock. Many techniques and tools are used to expose them. Chemicals may be used to dissolve the rock. It may be possible to brush or pick the rock material from around the fossil, but in hard rocks, hammers and chisels are used to chip away the matrix, or surrounding material. Many months, or even years, may be needed to complete the work.

Old geological map of rock distribution on both sides of the English Channel

Narrow chisel

Dusting brush

Toothbrush

FINE TOOLS

Small chisels will help when working close to the fossil. Brushes are used to dust away fragments of rock. Tough-bristled toothbrushes and water will remove dirt from robust fossil surfaces. Broken fragments of fossil can be carefully picked up with tweezers before sticking them together with adhesives. A hand lens may be used to view the fossil close up. Photos and notes of the work done may help in the future with similar fossils.

Fine tweezers

KEEPING RECORDS

Many books, both old and new, illustrate fossils found in particular localities or show the detailed differences among similar-looking specimens. These books can be consulted to help identify the fossils found. Some fossils may be very rare, so many books may need to be checked before the fossils can be identified. Labeled drawings of a fossil collection can make recognizing the shapes and details easier.

Fossil enamel surface

Root missing

Molar tooth of Gomphotherium

Tooth crown

FRAGILE FOSSILS

Fossils are often very delicate and fragile. Some can be stored quite easily in boxes, wrapped in tissue paper, but others, like this molar tooth of ancient elephant *Gomphotherium* (pp. 48–49), may need some attention first. Liquid plastics may be painted on the surface to strengthen the tooth by filling microscopic cracks.

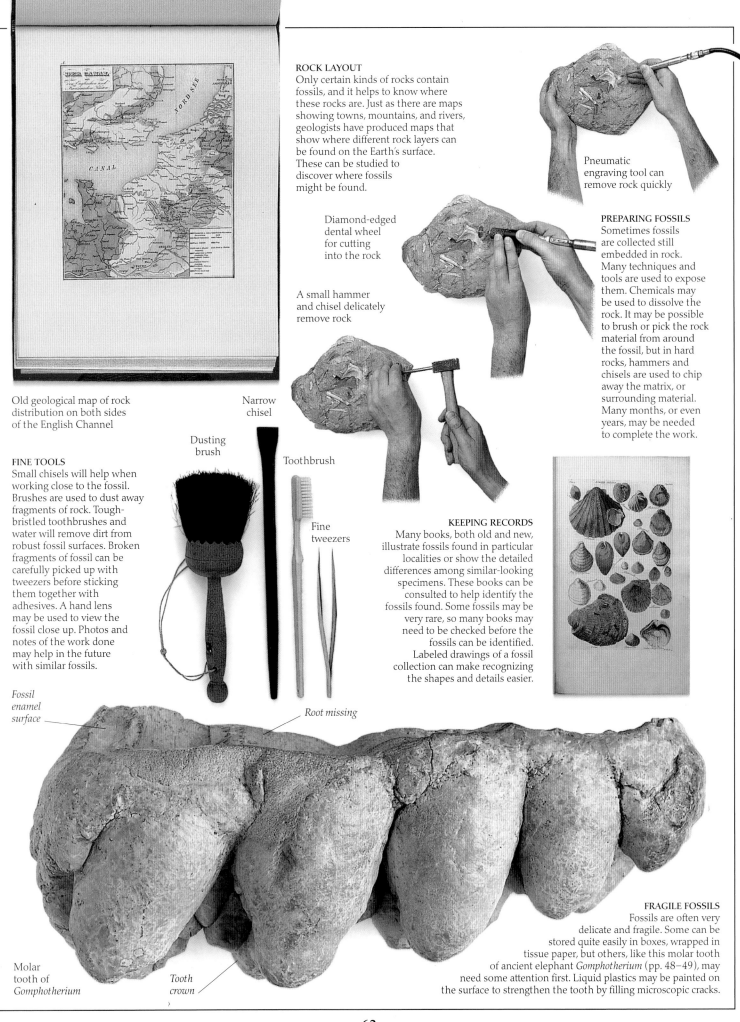

Tree of life

ALL ORGANISMS ON EARTH are related to each other, and all species share a common ancestor that lived billions of years ago. Humans, therefore, are related to every other life form. Understanding how organisms are related to each other is one of the main goals of biology. Paleontologists and other biologists are striving to piece together a complete tree of life—a pattern of relationships of all living and extinct organisms, equivalent to the family trees that many people use to trace their own family histories.

RELATEDNESS
Family trees, technically called cladograms, provide a way of classifying life and of tracing the path of evolution. Each branching point on this tree shows a leap in evolution—a new feature that makes a life form, and all of its descendants, distinctive. All the related life forms that share this feature (feathers, for instance), form a natural group, called a clade. Birds are an example of a clade. Grouping animals in clades shows how they are related, and how they evolved.

DINOSAURS

Birds

Nonbird dinosaurs

ARCHOSAURS

Caudipteryx

Crocodiles

Crocodile

DIAPSIDS

Lizards

Tiger

Mammals

TETRAPODS

Amphibians

Salamander

Lungfish

VERTEBRATES

DEUTEROSTOMES

Slender geophaguso

Ray-finned fish

Starfish

Echinoderms

BILATERIA

Blue-ringed octopus

Mollusks

PROTOSTOMES

Brachiopods

Arthropods

ANIMALIA

Australian spotted jellyfish

Jellyfish

Sponges

ANIMALS
All animals—from mammals and lizards to clams and sponges—share a common ancestor. Most animals can move from place to place and have complex cells containing miniature structures called organelles. Unlike plants, animals are incapable of making their own food. Instead, they must get their food by eating plants or other animals.

Stove-pipe sponge

BILATERIA
All animals, except for sponges, jellyfish, and corals, are bilaterians—they are descended from an ancestor that evolved bilateral symmetry. These symmetrical animals have a front and a back and an up side and a down side. This diagram of a beetle shows its plane of symmetry. Non-bilaterian animals, such as jellyfish and sponges, have either no symmetry or radial symmetry—they have an up side and down side but no front and back sides.

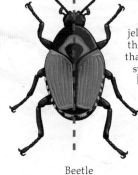
Beetle

DEUTEROSTOMES

The deuterostomes include the echinoderms and vertebrates, and these two seemingly very different animals share a major feature related to their development from an embryo. In both, the first opening in the embryo, called the blastopore, becomes the anus. So amazingly, the closest relatives of vertebrates are starfish and their kin. The other invertebrate animals, the protostomes, are much more distantly related.

White's tree frog, a vertebrate and a deuterostome

Vertebrate skull comprises more than 20 bones

VERTEBRATES

Vertebrates make up one of the most familiar groups of living and fossil organisms. All vertebrates possess a skeleton made out of bone and teeth made out of a hard substance called enamel. The earliest fossil vertebrates are over 500 million years old. For the first several million years of their evolution, vertebrates were restricted to the water. Later, the tetrapods evolved hands and feet and moved onto land, and then evolved into a vast array of species. Living vertebrates include over 100,000 species, most of which are fish.

Starfish are close relatives of vertebrates

Harbor seal

Arm has three main bones—humerus, radius, and ulna

Pelvic girdle provides a rigid support for the hind legs

Humerus

Radius

Fin ray

Humerus

Radius

Ulna

Ulna

Five digits

Bone structure of fin in ray-finned fish

Bone structure of fore limb in *Ichthyostega*, an early tetrapod

TETRAPODS

The tetrapods, or land-living vertebrates, evolved during the Devonian period, about 395 mya. Tetrapods have an important common characteristic—the presence of hands and feet with fingers and toes, which differ from the fins of their fishlike ancestors. Hands and feet allowed tetrapods to walk on land. Their robust rib cage and neck, which supported the head, also made these animals more stable on land. Today, tens of thousands of mammals, reptiles, amphibians, and birds represent living tetrapods.

Small brain case

Huge eye socket

Antorbital fenestra

Very large nasal chambers

Dinosaur tail was long and stiff, providing balance

Diplodocus skull

Long, flat lower jaw

ARCHOSAURS

Archosaurs, which in Greek means "ruling reptiles", include crocodiles, dinosaurs, and birds. This group emerged in the aftermath of the devastating Permian–Triassic mass extinction 250 mya and quickly rose to dominance. Archosaurs have many features in common, including a large, weight-saving space in front of the eyes called the antorbital fenestra. The fenestra may also have allowed archosaurs to breathe more efficiently.

Feathered wings of birds first evolved in nonflying dinosaurs

DINOSAURS

The most iconic and recognizable fossil species are surely the dinosaurs. They evolved during the Middle Triassic period (about 240 mya) and later diversified into a range of species, including giant carnivores and long-necked herbivores. Their descendants, the birds, remain successful today. In all dinosaurs, many features of the hind limb, such as an upright gait and a compact foot, enabled high speed and agility.

Alxasaurus, a feathered dinosaur

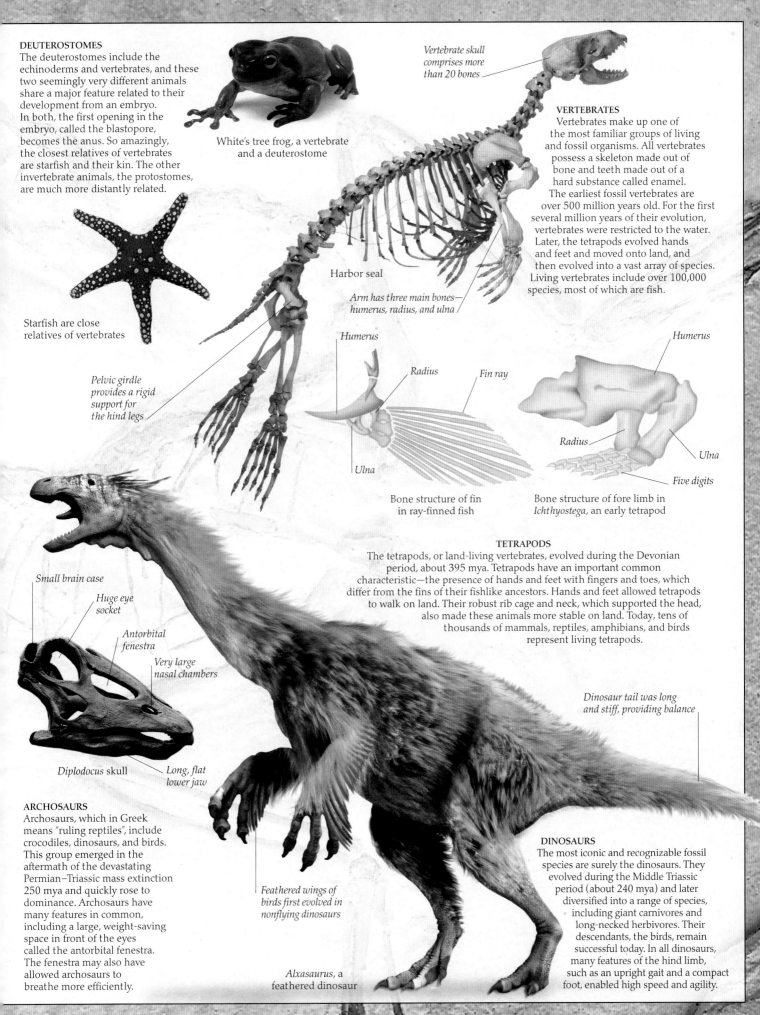

Diversity of life

THE HISTORY OF LIFE is the story of the birth of new species and the extinction of old ones. The overall diversity has risen and fallen ever since life began over 3 billion years ago. In general, diversity has steadily increased over much of geological history, but there have been five major mass extinctions that have killed organisms on a grand scale. Although the last such extinction, which killed the dinosaurs, was at the end of the Cretaceous period, human activity currently seems to be causing a sixth mass extinction.

MASS EXTINCTIONS
Mass extinctions are periods of time in which the rate of extinction of species is exceptionally great. There have been five mass extinction events in Earth's history. The largest of all, the Permian–Triassic extinction 250 mya, may have killed up to 95 percent of all species and produced a barren world in which only a few species survived. Most mass extinctions are probably caused by sudden events such as asteroid impacts or volcanic eruptions.

THE CURVE OF LIFE
This graph helps us understand the variation in the number of species on Earth over the past 542 million years. The history of life on our planet is dotted with periods when large numbers of species died out and periods when the numbers increased. Scientists use fossil records to study when a species lived. American scientist Jack Sepkoski (1948–99) studied thousands of individual fossils to measure diversity of life over time. He put all the data together and called it a "diversity curve."

Number of different life forms, or "genera"

3,000

2,000

1,000

0

Late Ordovician mass extinction

Late Devonian mass extinction

Period

| Cambrian | Ordovician | Silurian | Devonian | Carboniferous |

Time (mya) 542   488   444   416   359   299

THE FIRST ANIMALS
Sepkoski divided life into three great communities, or "faunas," which lived at different times. The first of these great faunas—the Cambrian Fauna—comprised mostly small, shelly fossils of uncertain identity and early members of living groups, such as arthropods and mollusks.

Opabinia, a puzzling sea-dwelling creature of the Cambrian

ANCIENT LIFE
The next great community, the Palaeozoic Fauna was dominated by invertebrate groups such as trilobites, crinoids, and brachiopods. During this time, the major invertebrates with two-part shells were brachiopods and not the bivalve mollusks (clams) that are common today. Many Paleozoic groups suffered devastating extinctions at the end of the Permian. Brachiopods and crinoids both survived, but in limited numbers, whereas the once-dominant trilobites disappeared completely.

Fossilized shell of the brachiopod *Cyclothyris difformis*

Trilobites

Crinoids

Brachiopods

Bivalve and gastropod mollusks

Ammonites

KEY   Period when a group thrived   Period when a group existed in small numbers

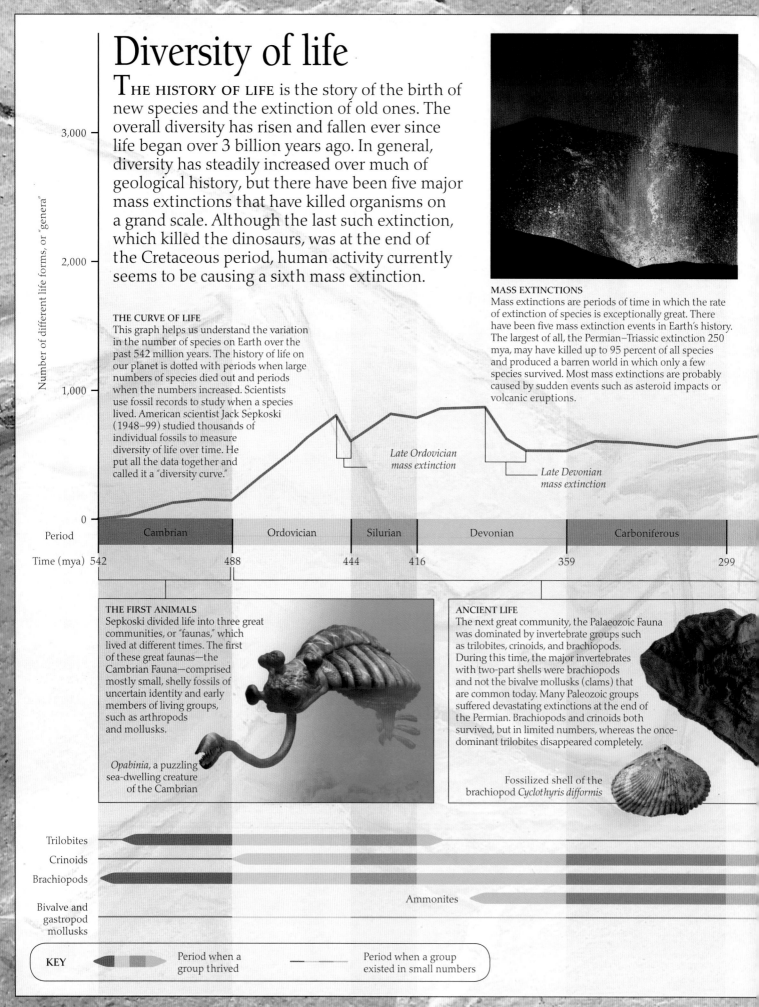

RISE OF DINOSAURS

The rise of dinosaurs during the early Mesozoic was one of the most profound events in the history of vertebrate evolution. Dinosaurs probably originated some time during the Middle Triassic period, approximately 240 mya. Over the next 50 million years, dinosaurs would gradually become more diverse, more abundant, and larger in size, before truly dominating Jurassic and Cretaceous ecosystems.

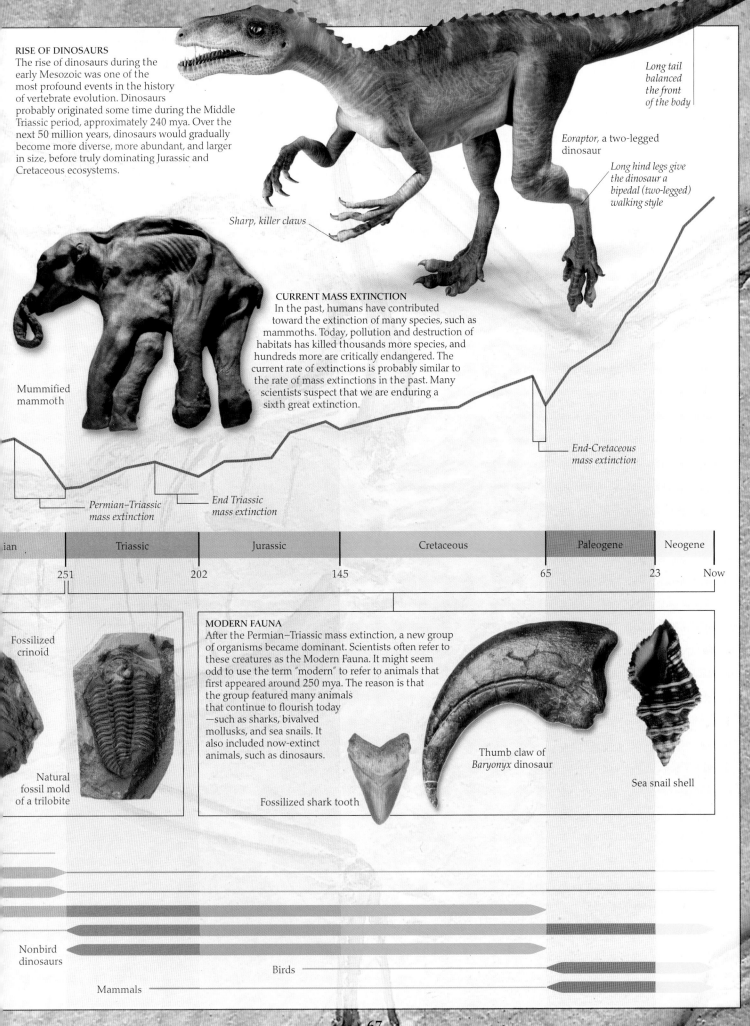

Long tail balanced the front of the body

Eoraptor, a two-legged dinosaur

Long hind legs give the dinosaur a bipedal (two-legged) walking style

Sharp, killer claws

CURRENT MASS EXTINCTION

In the past, humans have contributed toward the extinction of many species, such as mammoths. Today, pollution and destruction of habitats has killed thousands more species, and hundreds more are critically endangered. The current rate of extinctions is probably similar to the rate of mass extinctions in the past. Many scientists suspect that we are enduring a sixth great extinction.

Mummified mammoth

End-Cretaceous mass extinction

Permian–Triassic mass extinction

End Triassic mass extinction

...ian	Triassic	Jurassic	Cretaceous	Paleogene	Neogene
251	202	145	65	23	Now

MODERN FAUNA

After the Permian–Triassic mass extinction, a new group of organisms became dominant. Scientists often refer to these creatures as the Modern Fauna. It might seem odd to use the term "modern" to refer to animals that first appeared around 250 mya. The reason is that the group featured many animals that continue to flourish today —such as sharks, bivalved mollusks, and sea snails. It also included now-extinct animals, such as dinosaurs.

Fossilized crinoid

Natural fossil mold of a trilobite

Fossilized shark tooth

Thumb claw of *Baryonyx* dinosaur

Sea snail shell

Nonbird dinosaurs

Birds

Mammals

Earth over time

LITTLE ABOUT THE EARTH IS STATIC—continents collide and fragment, mountain ranges ascend toward the sky and then erode to dust, glaciers expand and contract, and oceans rise and fall. Drifting continents and changing climates have a profound influence on the evolution and distribution of living organisms. The story of the evolution of life and the changing Earth is intertwined, and it is a fascinating tale.

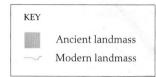

KEY

▨ Ancient landmass

〜 Modern landmass

THE BEGINNING

CHANGING TIMES
The Cambrian period was a time of rapid change. The existing continental mass split up, and three chunks separated from it—Laurentia, Baltica, and Siberia. These turned into large islands over millions of years. The separation also gave rise to the southern continent of Gondwana. In this period, no life existed on land, but animal diversity grew in the oceans suddenly and the ancestors of many invertebrate groups evolved at once.

A HUNTER
This shrimplike creature was one of the top predators in the Cambrian seas. *Anomalocaris* is a common fossil of the Burgess Shale fauna, and it probably used its large compound eyes to hunt by sight.

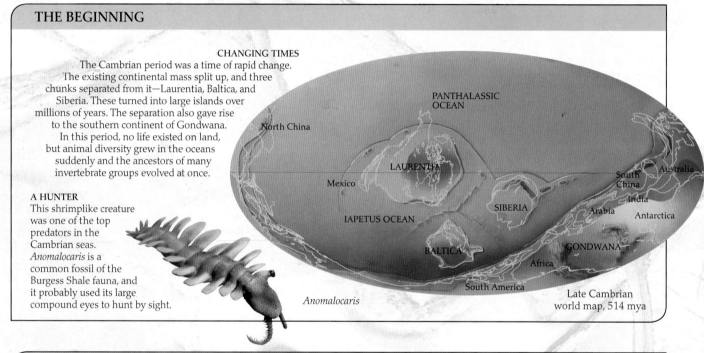

Anomalocaris

Late Cambrian world map, 514 mya

PANGAEA FORMS

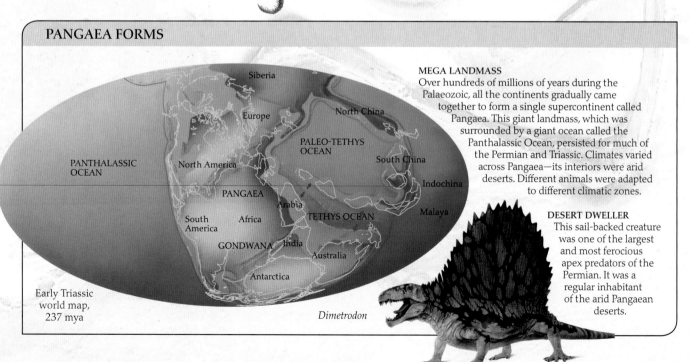

MEGA LANDMASS
Over hundreds of millions of years during the Palaeozoic, all the continents gradually came together to form a single supercontinent called Pangaea. This giant landmass, which was surrounded by a giant ocean called the Panthalassic Ocean, persisted for much of the Permian and Triassic. Climates varied across Pangaea—its interiors were arid deserts. Different animals were adapted to different climatic zones.

DESERT DWELLER
This sail-backed creature was one of the largest and most ferocious apex predators of the Permian. It was a regular inhabitant of the arid Pangaean deserts.

Early Triassic world map, 237 mya

Dimetrodon

PANGAEA SPLITS

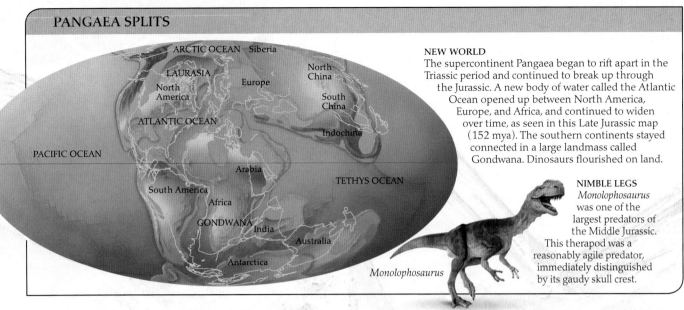

ARCTIC OCEAN Siberia
LAURASIA
North America
Europe
North China
South China
Indochina
ATLANTIC OCEAN
PACIFIC OCEAN
Arabia
South America
Africa
TETHYS OCEAN
GONDWANA
India
Australia
Antarctica

Monolophosaurus

NEW WORLD
The supercontinent Pangaea began to rift apart in the Triassic period and continued to break up through the Jurassic. A new body of water called the Atlantic Ocean opened up between North America, Europe, and Africa, and continued to widen over time, as seen in this Late Jurassic map (152 mya). The southern continents stayed connected in a large landmass called Gondwana. Dinosaurs flourished on land.

NIMBLE LEGS
Monolophosaurus was one of the largest predators of the Middle Jurassic. This therapod was a reasonably agile predator, immediately distinguished by its gaudy skull crest.

DRIFTING APART

BREAKING AWAY
The Cretaceous was an active time when the continents fragmented further. The southern continents—Africa, South America, Antarctica, and Australia—broke apart. One stretch of water split North America in two from the Arctic to the Gulf of Mexico, as seen in this Late Cretaceous map (94 mya). Organisms that once ranged across the entire supercontinent were split into populations on the separate landmasses. This promoted the formation of new species.

KILLERS AT SEA
The Cretaceous was a warm, humid world in which sea levels were very high. Large marine reptiles such as mosasaurs were the top predators in these seas.

Mosasaurus

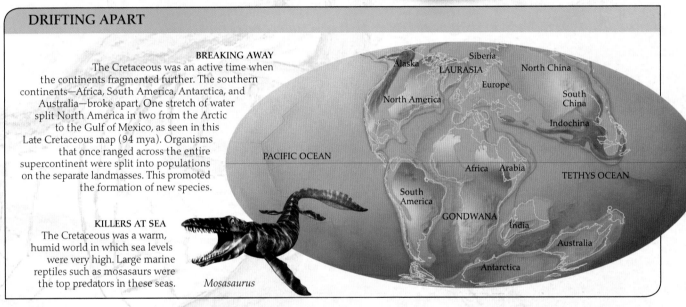

Alaska
Siberia
LAURASIA
North China
Europe
North America
South China
Indochina
PACIFIC OCEAN
Africa Arabia
TETHYS OCEAN
South America
GONDWANA
India
Australia
Antarctica

THE MODERN WORLD

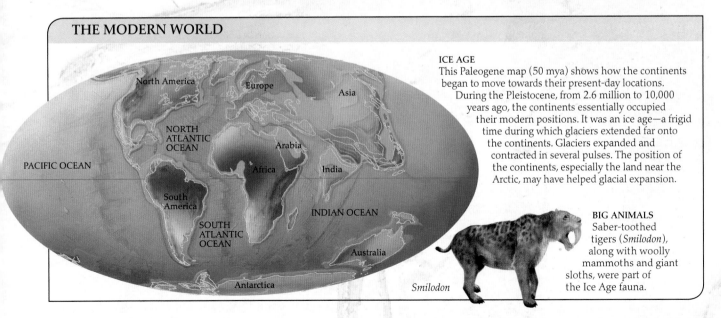

North America
Europe
Asia
NORTH ATLANTIC OCEAN
Arabia
PACIFIC OCEAN
Africa
India
South America
SOUTH ATLANTIC OCEAN
INDIAN OCEAN
Australia
Antarctica

Smilodon

ICE AGE
This Paleogene map (50 mya) shows how the continents began to move towards their present-day locations. During the Pleistocene, from 2.6 million to 10,000 years ago, the continents essentially occupied their modern positions. It was an ice age—a frigid time during which glaciers extended far onto the continents. Glaciers expanded and contracted in several pulses. The position of the continents, especially the land near the Arctic, may have helped glacial expansion.

BIG ANIMALS
Saber-toothed tigers (*Smilodon*), along with woolly mammoths and giant sloths, were part of the Ice Age fauna.

Glossary

AMMONITE
A mollusk, related to squid, that had a coiled, chambered shell and lived in Mesozoic seas.

AMNIOTIC EGG
An egg with an outer waterproof membrane. Inside, it is filled with fluid and allows an embryo to develop outside of the water without drying out.

AMPHIBIAN
A cold-blooded animal whose young use gills to breathe in water during the early stages of life and lungs to breathe on land as adults.

ARCHOSAUR
A land-living vertebrate with a space in the skull in front of the eye called an antorbital fenestra. Archosaurs originated 250 mya and include dinosaurs, birds, and crocodiles.

ARTHROPOD
An invertebrate animal with a hard external

Pachycephalosaurus,
a dinosaur

skeleton (exoskeleton), jointed limbs, and a body divided into segments. Living examples include spiders, crabs, and insects.

ASTEROID
A chunk of rock, ranging in size from a boulder to a miniature planet, that orbits the Sun. Asteroids sometimes crash into the Earth and other planets, and one such impact may have killed the dinosaurs 65 mya.

BIRD
A vertebrate animal with feathers, a wishbone, and an internal system of air sacs connected to the lungs. Most living birds have wings and can fly. Birds evolved from dinosaurs during the Mesozoic era.

BRACHIOPOD
A marine invertebrate with a two-part shell. Unlike a clam, both of its shell halves are symemetrical. Brachiopods evolved in the Cambrian, were very common during the Paleozoic, and are rare today.

CAMBRIAN EXPLOSION
The rapid appearance of many major animal groups in the fossil record 530 mya in the Cambrian period.

CARNIVORE
An animal that eats meat. Usually carnivores possess sharp teeth and claws with which they catch and process their prey.

CEPHALOPOD
A sea-living mollusk with large eyes, an internal or external shell, and a head ringed by tentacles. Living examples are octopus and squid.

COELACANTH
A lobe-finned fish, closely related to tetrapods, that was thought to be extinct but was found in the waters off South Africa in 1938.

DINOSAUR
A dominant terrestrial, herbivorous or carnivorous reptile, from the Mesozoic era. Dinosaurs had characteristic pelvic bone structures and most had upright hind limbs. Some dinosaurs were the evolutionary ancestors of birds.

EPOCH
An interval of time in the geological timescale that is smaller than a period. An example is the Pliocene.

ERA
An interval of time in the geological timescale, which groups together several periods. An example is the Mesozoic.

EURYPTERID
A large predatory arthropod that lived during the Paleozoic. They are commonly called "sea scorpions." However, they are not true members of the scorpion group.

Artist's impression of asteroid hitting Earth

EVOLUTION
The process by which life changes over time. This includes the transition from one species to another.

EXTINCTION
The dying out of a plant or animal species. The nonbird dinosaurs, for example, are extinct.

FOSSIL
The remains of something that was once alive, preserved in rock.

GENUS
A group of related species. In the classification of life, the genus groups together several species and several genera are then grouped together in a family.

GEOLOGIST
A scientist who studies the Earth, including the land, atmosphere, and oceans, with an aim to understand how our planet operates and how it has changed over time.

HERBIVORE
An animal that eats plants.

HABITAT
The area that is inhabited by a certain species of plant or animal. A species often has a usual habitat that has a certain climate or terrain.

HOMINID
A member of a family of primates, often called the "great apes," that includes humans, chimpanzees, gorillas, and orangutans.

Armored
millipede,
an invertebrate

HUMAN
A subgroup of hominid primates that is made up of the species *Homo sapiens* and several extinct relatives. Humans walk upright on two legs and have a large brain.

ICE AGE
A period of time during which global temperatures fall and large sheets of ice (glaciers) cover much of the land.

INVERTEBRATE
An animal, such as a clam, sponge, or jellyfish, without a backbone.

MAMMAL
An animal that is warm-blooded, covered in hair, and suckles its young.

MAMMOTH
A type of elephant with long tusks that lived during the Pliocene and Pleistocene. During the last ice age, some mammoths developed long hair, which helped them stay warm.

MARSUPIAL
A type of mammal whose young are born in an immature state and then climb into a pouch on the mother to continue developing.

MASS EXTINCTION
A time during which a larger than usual number of species becomes extinct. Most mass extinctions were probably rapid and caused by unexpected events such as asteroid impacts or large volcanic eruptions.

MESOZOIC
The era on the geological timescale, approximately 250–65 mya, that is often called the "Age of Dinosaurs."

Paleontologists at work

METEORITE
An object from outer space that has impacted the Earth's surface but stayed intact without disintegrating or turning into vapor.

NEANDERTHAL
A type of extinct human, closely related to living humans, that lived during the last ice age. Neanderthals were generally shorter and stockier than living humans.

ORNITHISCHIAN
One of a group of dinosaurs that have a pelvic bone structure similar to that of birds. Ornithischians have a pubis bone that points backward.

PALEONTOLOGIST
Someone who studies paleontology, the scientific study of ancient life, which is accomplished by studying fossils.

PALEOZOIC
The era on the geological timescale, approximately 542–250 mya that witnessed the origin of many major animal groups.

PEAT
An accumulation of partially decayed plants, which may later turn to coal over millions of years.

PERIOD
An interval of time in the geological timescale that is smaller than an era but larger than an epoch. An example is the Cretaceous.

Long, narrow wing supported by long fourth finger

Pterosaur

PLANT
An organism that produces its own food and has rigid cell walls surrounding its cells.

PLESIOSAUR
A sea-living reptile that lived during the Mesozoic and has a long neck and flippers used for fast swimming.

PREHENSILE
An organ that is adapted for grasping or holding, such as the hand of humans or the tail of many monkeys.

PRIMATE
A member of a group of mammals that includes monkeys, apes, and humans. Typical features include grasping hands and forward-facing eyes.

PTEROSAUR
A flying reptile of the Mesozoic era, which has a thin wing supported by an enormous finger.

REPTILE
A member of a group of animals that are covered in scales, generally cold-blooded, and reproduce by laying eggs.

SAURISCHIAN
A member of a major subgroup of dinosaurs, such as *Tyrannosaurus rex*, that has a pubis bone that projects forward.

SAUROPOD
A member of a subgroup of saurischian dinosaurs that has a long neck, small head, large belly, and columnar limbs. Sauropods were the largest animals ever to live on land.

SPECIES
A group of organisms that can reproduce with each other. In the classification of life, a species is one level below the genus.

STROMATOLITE
A moundlike structure formed by the trapping and binding of sediment by microorganisms such as cyanobacteria.

TAXONOMIST
A scientist who studies the relationship between ancestral organisms and their descendants.

TETRAPOD
A member of a major group of vertebrates that has hands and feet with fingers and toes. Often called the "limbed vertebrates," they are specialized for living on land.

TRILOBITE
A member of a major extinct subgroup of arthropods common in the Paleozoic and

Fossil of a trilobite

becoming extinct at the Permian–Triassic extinction.

VOLCANO
A fissure in the Earth's surface from which molten rock (lava) is released.

WHALE
A member of a group of mammals of the order Cetacea, distinguished from the smaller dolphins and porpoise. They have a fishlike body, flippers, and a head that is horizontally flattened.

Layers of cooled lava turned to rock

Reservoir of molten magma

Volcano

Index

AB

Acantherpestes, 23
Acanthostega, 25
Aegyptopithecus, 9, 54
Aepyornis, 53
Agassiz, Louis, 18
Aglaophyton, 22
algae 6–7, 12–13, 52
Allosaurus, 34–35
Alvarez, Luis and Walter, 60
Alxasaurus, 65
amber, 52
ammonites, 16, 53, 61, 70
amniotes, 28
amphibians, 7, 24–25, 28, 52, 70
angel fish 19
Anhanguera, 40
annalid worms, 12
Anning, Mary, 38
Anomalocaris, 68
apes, 54–55, 56
Archaeopteryx, 8, 42–3
archosaurs, 33, 64–65, 70
Arsinoitherium, 9, 46–47
Arthropleura, 23
arthropods, 7, 14, 20–23, 27, 70
Arvicola, 59
asteroids, 60, 70
Asteroxylon, 22
Australopithecus, 55–56
Barosaurus, 35
Baryonyx, 67
Basilosaurus, 47
bears, cave, 59
Belodon, 29
bilateria, 12
birds, 8, 28, 42–43, 53, 70
  first, 8, 42–43
  fossil feather, 43
Birkenia, 18
brachiopods, 6–8, 15–17, 61, 70
Burgess Shale, 6, 14–16

CDE

calcite, 16
Camarasaurus, 34
Cambrian period, 66, 68, 70
Canadaspis, 15
Canadia, 15
Cephalaspis, 7, 18
chondrites, 13
Citipati, 35
climate changes, 6–11, 58, 60
clubmosses, giant, 7, 26
coal, 7, 26–27
coelacanths, 19, 70
Coelodonta, 59
Coelophysis, 32
Collenia, 6
Compsognathus, 42
conodonts, 18
continents, 6–10
Cooksonia, 22
corals, 6, 16–17, 52
Cothurnocystis, 6, 16
creodonts 46
Cretaceous period 69
crinoids 7, 16
Cro-Magnons, 57, 59
cyanobacteria 12
cynodonts 30–31
Cynognathus 31
Dactylioceras 16
Daphoenus 47
Dart, Raymond 55
Deinotherium 9
Deltavjatia 29
deuterostomes 64–65
Dickinsonia 12
Dicynodon 30
dicynodonts 30–31
Didymograptus 61
Dimetrodon 28, 30–31, 68
Dimorphodon 41
dinosaurs 8, 32–37, 42, 44, 52–53, 61, 64–65, 67, 70
Diplodocus 32–33, 35, 65
Diplomystus 19
Diprotodon 50
Dipterus 24
dodo 61
Dromaeosaurus 34
Dsungaripterus 41
Dunkleosteus 20–21
Earth, formation of 6, 10–11
Edaphosaurus 28
Ediacara 6, 12, 14, 16
elephants 9, 48–49
Eomaia 44
Eoraptor 32, 67
Eryops 33
eukaryotes 12–13
Euoplocephalus 37
Eurypterus 20
evolution 64–67, 70
extinction 7, 8, 60–61, 66–67, 70

FGH

ferns 26, 28
fish
  bony 18–19, 20
  jawed 7, 18, 20–21
  jawless 7, 18
  lobe-finned 24
footprints 10, 34, 55, 62
fossils 70
  as evidence 106
  collecting 62–63
  formation of 11
fruit 53
fungi 12
fur 44–45
Gallimimus 33
geological periods 68–69, 71
Gigantopithecus 55
Gigantoscorpio 23
Gillicus 20
Glyptodon 51
Gomphotherium 48, 63
Gondwanaland 6–7
graptolites 61
Hallucigenia 15
hedgehogs, 45
Herrerasaurus 32
Heterodontosuarus 33
Hipparion 49
Hippopotamus 59
Holophagus 19
hominids 54–57, 70
Homo erectus 56–57
Homo habilis 9, 56–57
Homo sapiens 56
horses 8, 45, 49, 51
horsetails 26
humans 9, 55–57, 70
Hyaenodan 46
Hypsilophodon 37
Hyracotherium 8, 49

IJKL

ice ages 6, 9, 18, 58–59, 69, 70
ichthyosaurs 8, 38, 52
Ichthyostega 24–5, 65
Iguanodon 33
insects 22–23, 42
invertebrates 12–17, 70
Iridium 60
ivy 58
Jurassic period, 8, 69
Karroo Basin 11, 31
Ketophyllum 17
Lake Mungo 57
Latimeria 19
Leakey, Louis and Mary 55, 56, 57
LepidodenDron 7, 26–27
Lepidotes 19
Leptictidium 8
lungfish 24
Lystrosaurus 30

MN

magnolia 60
Maiasaura 52–53
mammals 8–9, 28, 31, 44–51, 52, 58–61, 71
mammoths 9, 58, 67, 71
Marrella 14
marsupials 50, 51, 71
mass extinctions 7, 8, 60–61, 66–67, 71
mastodons 9, 48, 63
Mawsonites 6
Megaloceros 60–61
Megatherium 51
Megazostrodon 8, 44
Megistotherium 46
Merychippus 49
Mesodma 44
mesosaurs 29
Mesozoic era 71
Messel quarry 45
meteorites 11, 13, 60–61, 71
Meyer, Herman von 43
Miller, Dr. Stanley 13
millipedes 23, 28
Moeritherium 48
mollusks 6, 7, 18, 53
Monolophosaurus 69
Morganucodon 44
Mosasaurus 39, 69
Moschops 30
mountains 6–7, 10, 14
  Himalayas 9–10
  Rocky Mountains 14
Neanderthals 56–57, 71
  Kebara Cave 57
  La Ferrassie Cave 57
  Neander Valley 57
Neoceratodus 24

OPQ

Olduvai Gorge 56
omnivores 8
Opabinia 66
orangutans 54
ornithiscians 36–37, 71
Ornithocheirus 40–41
Ornithosuchus 33
Oviraptor 35, 53
Oxynoticeras 53
Palaeoniscum 8, 45
Paleozoic era 66, 68, 71
Pangaea 7, 8, 50, 68, 69
Panthera 58
Parasaurolophus 36
pareiasaurs 29
pelycosaurs 28, 30
Phiomia 48–49
Phorusrhacus 43
Pikaia 14
placentals 50–51
placoderms 18, 20–21
placodonts 39
Placodus 39
plants 7–8, 10, 11, 12, 22, 71
Plateosaurus 35
plate tectonics 10
plesiosaurs 38–39, 71
pliosaurs 39
polychaete worms 15
primates 9, 54, 71
proboscideans 9, 48–49
Procolophon 11, 29
Proconsul africanus 54
Prolibytherium 46
Protacarus 22
Protostega 38–39
Pteranodon 41
Pterichthyodes 18, 21
Pterodactylus 41
pterosaurs 8, 40–41, 71
Pterygotus 20
Ptilodus 44
Quetzalcoatlus 40–41

RST

reproduction
  algae 52
  amniotic egg 28, 52, 70
  budding coral 52
  eggs 7, 24, 52
  live birth 8, 38, 52
  marsupial 44
  mating flies 52
  placental 44
  pollen 60
  sexual 52
  tadpole 52
reptiles 7–8, 11, 52, 71
  dinosaurs 32–37
  first 7, 28
  flying 40–41, 61
  mammal-like 30–31
marine 20, 38–39, 61
primitive 11, 29
rhamphorhynchoids 29, 40
Rhamphorhyncus 40
Rhynchosaurus 29
Rhynie Chert 22
Rhyniella 22
rocks 6–7, 10–11, 62–63
saurischians 34–35, 71
scorpions 7, 23, 28
sea, early life in 6–10, 16–21
sharks 7, 21, 67
Sivapithecus 54
Sivatherium 47
Smilodon 9, 51, 69
Solnhofen Limestone 40, 41–42
species 66–67, 71
sponges 14, 16, 64
Spriggina 12
Stegoceras 36
Stegodon 48–49
Stegosaurus 37
Stenopterygius 8, 38, 52
Stereosternum 29
Sternberg, George 21
Stethacanthus 21
Sthenurus 50
stromatolites 6, 12, 71
swamps, forest 7, 26–27
teleosts 18, 20–21
Tertiary period 69
Tetrahedraletes 22
tetrapods 24–25, 60, 64–65, 71
Thrinaxodon 31
Thylacinus 50
Thylacosmilus 51
Tiktaalik 24
Toxodon 51
tree of life 64–65
Triceratops 37
trilobites 6–8, 10–11, 16, 17, 20, 71
Tuojiangosaurus 36–37
turtles, giant 38–39
Tyrannosaurus rex 8, 34–35

UVWX

Uintatherium 45
vertebrates 18–19, 64–65
volcanoes 6, 10, 71
voles 59
Westlothiana 7, 28–29
whales, 47, 71
Wiwaxia 15
worms 12, 14, 15
Xiphactinus 20–21

Acknowledgments

Dorling Kindersley would like to thank:
The Trustees of the National Museums of Scotland, Dr. Tim Smithson, and Dr. Michael Coates (University of Cambridge) for their valuable assistance on making the model of *Westlothiana*. For help on research and photography: Dr. Ian Rolfe, Dr. Bobbie Paton, Bill Baird, Bob Reekie, and Dr. Sheila Brock, National Museums of Scotland; Dr. Neil Clark, Hunterian Museum; Dr. Ken Joysey, Dr. M. Coates, Dr. Jenny Clack, Ray Symonds, and Sarah Finney, Zoology Museum; Dr. Robin Cocks, Dr. Jerry Hooker, Sandra Chapman, Andy Currant, Valerie Harris, Peter Whybrow, Robert Kruszynski, Ann Lum, Helen Santler, and Tim Parmenter, Natural History Museum; Dr. David Norman, Dr. Simon Conway Morris, Dr. Barry Rickards, Mike Dorling, Rod Long, and Margaret Johnston, Sedgwick Museum; Alastair Gunning and Patricia Bascombe, Glasgow Museum Services; P. Chadwick, A. Crawford, J. Downs, L. Gardiner, S. Gorton, C. Keates, D. King, M. Long, and A. Neimenn for extra photography. For kind permission to photograph: *Acanthostega* and *Ichthyostega*, Geological Museum, University of Copenhagen, Denmark; *Sinokannemeyeria*, Paul Howard, Yorkshire Museum and Ian O'Riordan, Edinburgh City Art Centre; *Skakoper cryptozoan*, Leicester University Geological Dept.; Model of woolly mammoth, Royal British Columbia Museum, Victoria, Canada. For design and editorial assistance: Manisha Patel, Sharon Spencer, Helena Spiteri, and Scott Steedman. **Model maker** John Holmes; **Artwork** Simone End, William Lindsay, and John Woodcock; **Proofreading** Lili Bryant and Caitlin Doyle; **Index** Helen Peters.

Picture credits
The publisher would like to thank the following for their kind permission to reproduce their photographs:
(Key: a-above; b-below/bottom; c-center; f-far; l-left; r-right; t-top)
Bayerische Staatssammlung fur Palaontologie und Historische Geologie, Munich 41tr, 41br. Bettmann Archive 13tl, 14cl. Biofotos/Stames Summerhays 52c. Dr. Neil Clark 18cl, 21bl. Cleveland Museum of Natural History, Ohio 21tl. Dr. Michael Coates 25tr. Bruce Coleman Ltd. 12tl, 17cr; H. Reinhard 22tc; Jane Burton 28tl, 43cr; V. Serventy 50br; John Canoclosi 62c. By permission of W. W. Norton & Co. Ltd. and Marianne Collins 14tr, 15tl. Simon Conway Morris 6c, 12c, 12bc, 12cr, 14cr, 14bc, 15tr, 15c, 15cl, 15bc. **Corbis:** Louie Psihoyos/Science Faction 71cl. **Dorling Kindersley:** Natural History Museum, London 66fbr; Sedgwick Museum of Geology, Cambridge 67bl; Weymouth Sea Life Centre 64c, 64crb. © Crown copyright 62tr. Mary Evans Picture Library 20tl, 53tc, 59br. FLPA/S Johnson 10tr, 44tr. Geological Society 38tl. **Geological Survey of Greenland, Copenhagen:** A. A. Garde 11br. Glasgow Museums 26–27b. Robert Harding Picture Library 10c. Dr. Gillian King, **South African Museum:** C. Booth 30bl; R. M. H. Smith 31cr. Paul McCready, AeroVironment Inc. 40cl. © Trustees of the National Museums of Scotland 1994 22tl, 22bc. The Natural History Museum, London 8br, 13bl, 22tr, 30bc, 31c, 40tr, 43tr, 44br, 45tl, 46c, 47cr, 49tr, 50tr, 51tr, 57c, 58tl, 59tc. Novosti Photo Library 58bc. Oxford Scientific Films 52bl. Planet Earth Pictures/Peter Scooner 19tc. Science Photo Library 18tl; Ludek Pasek 24tl, 27tl; Martin Dohrn 41cr; John Reader 55tr, 55br, 56tl; Roger Ressmeyer Starlight 60cl; Prof. Walter Alvarez 60bc; NASA 61tl; US Navy 61tc; David A. Hardy 61br. Forschungsinstitut und Naturmuseum Senckenberg, Frankfurt 44–45c. Paul C. Sereno 32tr. Wojciech Skarzynski 33br. Sternberg Museum, Hays, Kansas 20br, 21cr. Texas Memorial Museum, The University of Texas at Austin, courtesy Prof. Wann Langston Jr. 40–41bc. Dr. P. Wellnhofer 40cl, 40bl, 42bl, 43c. Dr. R. T. Wells, Flinders University, photographer F. Coffa 50cl.

Wall chart: Corbis: Bettmann fcla; **Dorling Kindersley:** Trustees of the National Museums of Scotland fbl, clb, cb, fcl/(crinoid), Hunterian Museum (University of Glasgow) fclb, fcrb, Natural History Museum, London bl, fbr, crb, fcr, fcr/(Hipparion), fcra, Royal British Columbia Museum, Victoria, Canada, c, Sedgwick Museum of Geology, Cambridge ftl/(trilobite).

Jacket images: *Front:* **Dorling Kindersley:** Hunterian Museum (University of Glasgow) ftl; Natural History Museum, London ca; Royal British Columbia Museum, Victoria, Canada (main image); Royal Museum of Scotland, Edinburgh tc. **Science Photo Library:** Martin Dohrn / Stephen Winkworth cla. *Back:* **Dorling Kindersley:** Natural History Museum, London tl, cra, bc; Royal Museum of Scotland, Edinburgh l; University Museum of Zoology, Cambridge cl.

All other images © Dorling Kindersley
For further information, see: **www.dkimages.com**